A Teacher's Guide to

Interactive Writing

Grades PreK–2

A Teacher's Guide to

Interactive Writing

Grades PreK–2

MATT HALPERN

HEINEMANN ▸ **PORTSMOUTH, NH**

Heinemann
145 Maplewood Avenue, Suite 300
Portsmouth, NH 03801
www.heinemann.com

Offices and agents throughout the world

LCCN is on file with the Library of Congress.
ISBN: 978-0-325-13241-9

Acquisitions Editor: Zoë Ryder White
Production Editor: Kimberlee Sims
Cover and Interior Designer: Monica Ann Cohen
Cover and Interior Art: © 2019 Zapatosoldador/Shutterstock (grass, sky, sun); Monica Ann Cohen
Cover and Interior Photography: Carrie Garcia
Typesetter: Monica Ann Cohen
Manufacturing: Val Cooper
Video Production: Rene Preston, Lori Andrews, Carrie Garcia, Lee Vandergrift, Jeff Cannon, Lauren Litton, Sherry Day, Heather O'Bryan, Michael Grover, Paul Tomasyan, Dennis Doyle

Printed in the United States of America on acid-free paper

1 2 3 4 5 MPP 27 26 25 24 23   PO 4500871455

To teachers
everywhere—
you inspire me
with your bravery
and open hearts.

Book Map

Section One

Welcome to Interactive Writing 1

Section Two

The Predictable Flow of an Interactive Writing Session 33

Video Contents

Section Three

To access the videos for *A Teacher's Guide to Interactive Writing*:

1. Go to **http://hein.pub/Interactive-login**.

2. Log in with your username and password. If you do not already have an account with Heinemann, you will need to create an account.

3. On the Welcome page, choose "Click here to register an Online Resource."

4. Register your product by entering the code **INTERWRIT** (be sure to read and check the acknowledgment box under the keycode).

5. Once you have registered your product, it will appear alphabetically in your account list of My Online Resources.

Note: When returning to Heinemann.com to access your previously registered products, simply log in to your Heinemann account and click on "View my registered Online Resources."

Acknowledgments

TO MY TWO BRILLIANT (AND PATIENT) EDITORS:
Katie Wood Ray, you took a chance on me and helped me create a vision for this book and start writing! Zoë Ryder White, you came to me when I needed you most. Your dedication, conversation, and friendship mean the world to me. It is not an understatement to say I could not have written this book without both of you amazing ladies. I will forever be grateful.

To the wonderful folks at Heinemann who have helped me on this journey and made it all possible: Kim Cahill, Sherry Day, Jaclyn Karabinas, Karen Short, Edie Davis Quinn, Heather O'Bryan, Catrina Swasey, Monica Ann Cohen, Kime Sims, Val Levy, Michael Grover, Paul Tomasyan, Dennis Doyle, Lori Andrews (HMH), Lee Vandergrift (HMH), Carrie Garcia (HMH), Rene Preston (HMH), and Lauren Litton (HMH).

To the brilliant educational minds that have influenced and inspired me throughout the years. If you've ever written a professional book, I probably have read and been inspired and for that, thank you!

To the folks who have mentored me, directly or indirectly: Lori Elliott, LaNesha Tabb, Deedee Wills, Susan Dee, Kristi Mraz, Paul France, Pat Douglass, Maggie Roberts, Liz Kleinrock, M. Colleen Cruz, Jennifer Serravallo, and Matt Glover—thank you all for your inspiration and encouragement.

To every single educator I've ever worked with, thank you for helping me see, understand, listen, reflect, learn, grow, and be the best educator I can be.

To every child I've had the honor of teaching. As you know, once you're my student, you're always my student. I've seen many of you grow up, go to college, get married, and become the amazing adults I knew you'd be when you were amazing little ones. You each have taught me more than I could ever teach you. Always remember, Mr. Halpern loves you.

To my social media friends, if you're someone I've connected with on Facebook, Instagram, or Twitter, thank you for your support, help, and guidance, and for being a safe place to take risks and learn. A special shout out to Jillian Starr and Nate Lyon, who have become dear friends online and in real life.

To all my friends who have believed and supported me, thank you! Having friends truly makes life sweeter. Karen Robbie and Emily Frizzel-Day, both of you have helped me,

personally and professionally, more than you'll ever know. I love you both to the moon and back!

To my writing muses. Maggie Knowles and Elize Vaz, you two truly pushed me to write when I didn't think I had it in me and for that I am forever grateful.

To my family, Mom, Jill, Amy, and Mickey, thank you ALL for supporting and believing in me! And to my grandparents, Jean and Ted, thank you both. I hope you're looking down from above and feeling proud.

To Dave, how do you thank someone for helping you be the highest version of yourself? Without you, I simply wouldn't be who I am today. Your support, love, and friendship have made me a better teacher, friend, and person. Thank you from the bottom of my heart.

Take a Leap!

MY FIRST YEAR AS A CLASSROOM TEACHER, AS I WAS SETTING UP
the room, I remember my first thought was "How can I make my classroom the most inviting place for my students?" Yes, I had much to learn, but my heart was in the right place. Wanting my students to feel welcome and comfortable was important to me and buying "all the stuff" seemed like a good way to do it. I spent more time than I'd like to admit searching, buying, and decorating the room. The appearance of the classroom meant so much to me, but why? When I think back to "first year teacher Matt" I remember thinking:

* If the classroom looks nice, families and students will see I care.

* If I have all the "stuff" in my classroom, I'll be ready for anything!

* If I find just the right "stuff," nothing will shake me!

Looking back, I realize all the unknowns about teaching were so scary, and I was looking for some things I could control. So many unknowns. My anxiety was high and the classroom environment was something I could tackle—even before any students walked into the room. What I quickly learned was no matter how cute and put together my classroom was, all the scary unknowns still existed. There had to be other ways to build community and nurture student agency. This realization became the seed of me starting to let go.

It took me a few years to understand the only thing I am truly in control of in (and out of) the classroom is myself. This "letting go" allowed me to start looking for more and more ways to relax my practice and let my students have voice, choice, and ownership over their learning and environment. I was lucky enough to work at Project Based Learning school for a few years. PBL introduced me to the importance of student voice and choice and piqued my interest in how I could further let go. My search led me to

books and those books led me to authors. One who particularly inspired my work with students was the amazing Kristi Mraz.

After reading her books and following her online, one day, by chance (and a little bit of work), I found myself walking into her classroom. I was there with a small group doing a site visit as part of a Teacher's College Institute. As I walked around Kristi's classroom, the amount of student print up on the walls was simply astounding. I don't think there was one piece of paper up in the classroom that didn't have some sort of student writing or drawing on it. Her classroom was a directive to me: Do more. Do Better. Step up.

I walked out of Kristi's classroom determined to make a shift in the amount of ownership my students took in *their* classroom space. That was the shift. This isn't my classroom. It's theirs. How can I hand over the keys to the space? I had to get my kids writing more, creating more, and to do that, I had to reflect on my teaching and find opportunities for shifts.

Interactive writing provided the perfect canvas for student-created writing, tools, charts, and yes, even decorations. To be clear, I am working right along with my students, so I have a hand in the writing too, but children are always centered in the process. Once I shifted to starting the school year with a classroom devoid of almost any writing or decorations, the possibilities became almost limitless. There are a few signs for adults stating, "Student-created work coming soon!" and that is about it. In the first few weeks of school students help create our schedule, calendar, rules, and a few anchor charts. The simple act of waiting for students to arrive is transformative.

The icing on the cake is the community cultivated from the interaction that shared experience fosters. By thinking through obstacles, being persistent and brave, and celebrating successes and wins *together*, we build and strengthen the trust and understanding that form the foundation for learning. Quite simply, interactive writing is a pivotal piece of our learning community.

What I have learned is you have to take a leap of faith. I'm reminded of the scene in *Indiana Jones and the Last Crusade* when Indiana sees a giant chasm in front of him with no clear path across. He stands there, sweating, unsure of what to do until finally, he closes his eyes, puts one foot forward, and takes a leap of faith. The path is there, right under him, only he couldn't see it. Only after he took a deep breath and waited did it appear. Interactive writing feels a little like that at first. When you feel ready and energized, it feels *less* like that. My hope is this book will help you feel prepared. Your students can do it. You can do it. Take a breath and take a leap with me.

VIDEO I.1: *Including Students in the Creation of Their Environment*

Welcome to Interactive Writing

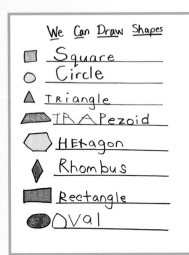

We Can Draw Shapes

Square
Circle
Triangle
TRAPezoid
HExagon
Rhombus
Rectangle
Oval

I wanted this chart to be made quickly, so I drew most of the shapes ahead of time, but I also wanted to do some informal assessing of students' understanding of shape names, so I left a few off to draw with them.

I use a sentence stem to get their conversations going and promote talking in full sentences.

I honor their ideas, and then I offer words that capture those ideas and make sense for the task at hand.

This simple invitation to interact with my teaching helps students stay engaged.

I say the word clearly and nod my head once as I do.

SCHOOL HAS BEEN IN SESSION FOR A FEW DAYS. I SIT IN FRONT OF my class at the easel, prepared to make a chart about drawing shapes.

Me: We've been learning about shapes. I thought we could make a chart to show all the names of shapes we're learning to draw.

With magnets, I hang up a piece of large paper that shows a few shapes—a circle, triangle, rhombus—drawn down the left-hand side. The first shape has yet to be drawn on the chart and no text is on the paper. The dramatic "reveal" of the paper is intentional—this is important work; it deserves a little fanfare.

Me: What should we call our chart? Take thirty seconds and talk to your partner about some ideas. Our chart could be called . . .

As children chat with their partners on the carpet, I listen in, and then I bring them back together.

Me: I heard some fantastic ideas—Shapes We Know, Drawing Shapes. What if we called our chart "We Can Draw Shapes!"?

Heads begin to nod and a few children shout "yes!" I write We Can Draw Shapes! on the top of the paper.

Me: I'm going to draw the first shape. See if you know what it's called. When you think you know it, put your finger on your forehead.

I slowly draw a square and fingers start popping up to temples. As I finish the square, I ask the group . . .

Me: . . . and this shape is called a . . .

Class: Square!

Me: Now, I want to write the word "square" next to it. Square. How many words do you hear?

Class: One!

Me: Yes, one word, so I'll draw one line for it.

Me: Now, I need a friend to come up and help me write the word square. ◄

VIDEO 1.1: *Setting the Scene for Interactive Writing*

I glance out at the group. Even though we've only been in school a few days, we've done this a few times already, so they know I'm looking for active, engaged learners. They also know I'm thinking carefully about who to call up.

My language is intentional. I use writing instead of making or drawing to send an important message: We are writers!

Me: Sam, why don't you come up? ◄

Sam perks up and in a few seconds joins me at the easel. I hand him the marker.

I select Sam because his name starts with the same letter and sound as square. I also know Sam needs practice writing the letter S.

Me: Square. Let's say it slowly and think about the sound we hear first. Sssquaaarrr. ◄

Class, including Sam: S!

Students who are ready join me in saying the word slowly, hearing multiple sounds beyond the first. I'm laying the foundation for transfer to independent writing.

Sam: I have an S at the beginning of my name! ◄

Me: Do you need help writing the S?

Sam: No! I write it every time I write my name! ◄

This is why I picked Sam. I know he writes this letter often, but also could use some direct instruction and practice.

Me: Class, let's write an S with Sam. Get your fingers ready. Write an S in the air with me as Sam writes it on the paper.

His confidence is affirming, so I won't over-scaffold, but I will give some guidance to him and the class with this tricky letter.

I point to the left-most part of the line I've drawn and nod at Sam to begin.

This nonverbal cue is a reminder that we read and write from left to right.

Me: Draw a C up high, then curve around. ◄

Me: What a sensational S, Sam!

I watch both Sam and the class. I am informally assessing throughout the process.

I motion for the marker back and nod for Sam to take his spot on the rug.

While I write the rest of the letters, I say them aloud and the children make their best attempts to write them in the air.

Me: Now I'll write the rest of the word: q, u, a, r, e, square!

Me: Now, let's look at the next shape.

VIDEO 1.2:
Interactive Writing vs. Shared Writing

What Is Interactive Writing?

Interactive writing is a fluid, flexible, engaging teaching tool used to model reading and writing skills and strategies while sharing the pen with students. As you can see in this scene, in a relatively small amount of instructional time I am teaching students about letters, sounds, and concepts of print. With interactive writing, these literacy skills are always in play, but because you can compose text about math, science, social studies—really any topic at all—the teaching can extend well beyond literacy. Over time, the practice becomes so routine that children know what to do and expect and you will see opportunities for interactive writing everywhere.

Whether with the whole class, a small group, or an individual child, the experience of interactive writing—especially at the beginning of the year—can be truly magical. Letters, words, and sentences appear as children come up to share the pen. For many beginning writers who are still reluctant to try and write on their own, it seems almost impossible that we're able to create text, but we do . . . together. And with each experience, their confidence grows.

Importantly, interactive writing is a powerful tool to scaffold children's literacy skills toward *independence*. The goal is to have scaffolding go from heavier to leaner as the year progresses. If we want our students to become independent readers and writers, we must give them lots of opportunities to work with us and then transfer their learning into reading and writing workshops.

> **Sharing the pen is not simply a ritual . . . the actions have high instructional value.**
> (McCarrier, Fountas, and Pinnell 2000)

A Photo Tour of Interactive Writing

Interactive writing is not a time for students to sit at desks or tables. It's not quiet. It's not rigid. It's not predictable. It's a time for writing to come alive as children share the thinking work of writing and share the pen with their teacher. The scope of what we cover is vast but necessary during this formative time of children's writing development. Here are some of the key concepts and skills interactive writing helps us with:

- ❋ Print carries meaning
- ❋ Print goes from left to right
- ❋ Return sweep
- ❋ The difference between letters and words
- ❋ How letters make sounds and words
- ❋ How to form letters and leave spaces
- ❋ How to come up with ideas and put those ideas on paper
- ❋ How letters can work together
- ❋ How certain words can help us read and write many others.

To give you a feeling for how this plays out in the classroom, let's go on a little photo tour of some interactive writing from the first few months of school in my classroom.

VIDEO 1.3: *Matt's Video Tour of Interactive Writing from the First Few Months of School*

Kindergarten Class Schedule

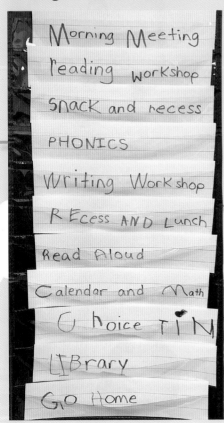

Morning Meeting
reading workshop
Snack and recess
PHONICS
Writing Workshop
REcess AND Lunch
Read Aloud
Calendar and Math
Choice TIM
LIBrary
Go Home

First-Grade Class Schedule

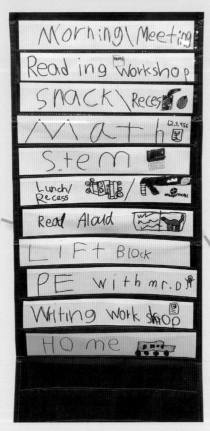

Morning\Meeting
Reading Workshop
Snack\Recess
Math
Stem
Lunch/Recess
Read Aloud
LIFt Block
PE with mr.D
Writing work shop
HOme

Class Rules

With interactive writing, I'm able to meet each child exactly where they are by offering a unique experience for each learner as they come up to share the pen. On this chart, for example, the child who wrote *words* started kindergarten with a grasp of most letter sounds and the ability to write both upper and lowercase letters. I helped the child who wrote *KIND* stretch out the sounds, but at this point he was most comfortable writing uppercase letters. The child who wrote just the L in *Listener* and *Learner* needed a lot of scaffolding, so I wrote the L with a yellow marker and he traced it (in *Listener*) and then we used hand-over-hand to write *Learner*.

CLASS Rules
1. My Body I2 gentle.
2. My Words are KIND.
3. I am a Good Listener.
4. I am a BRAve Learner.

During the first days of kindergarten, I work with my students to create our schedule. The scaffolding is high, with me offering a lot of hand-over-hand (with the child's consent, the teacher places their hand on top of the student's hand, holding the marker to guide them in writing the letter), giving models of letter formations, and directly telling letters and sounds. The message is, *print carries meaning.* As we study environmental print, we begin to create our own. In the second example, first graders, with more skills and writing experience behind them, do most of the writing and drawing to create their schedule.

A Teacher's Guide to Interactive Writing

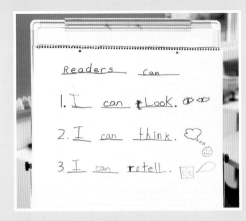

Anchor charts record important content we are learning together. On this chart, the children wrote a simple repeating word, *I*. A child wrote *can* in the title of the chart, and then I wrote it each additional time in the chart to save time.

Labels Around the Classroom

I release some of the scaffolding by having children work in partnerships and small groups to label things around the classroom as I circulate and coach in. The partnerships are purposeful because I make sure students with different skills work together. The children use alphabet charts to say words and write the sounds they hear, and over time their inventive spelling includes more and more sounds (the digraphs and blends they are noticing in their reading, for example).

By October, we're learning high-frequency words and using them in our interactive writing (e.g., *a*, *it*, *on*, *the*). As letter sound knowledge increases, I let more of the scaffolding down and children approximate spelling for more words.

Labeled Diagrams

This interactive writing lesson allows children to work on a variety of skills. CVC words (e.g., *cup, rug, bed, box*) and handwriting (the d in *bed* was corrected). As I call individuals up to work with me, students have their own pictures to label on clipboards.

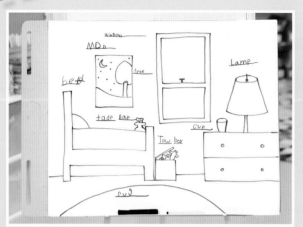

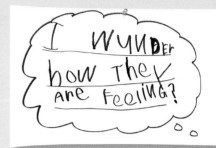

As we prepare for our open house, we write a welcome note to families. Because the audience for this piece is outside the immediate classroom community, I coach into conventional spelling and do some of the writing as well (see Section Two, page 56).

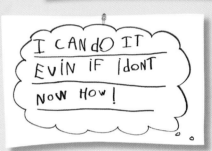

An invitation to our stuffed animals for a day of learning, this piece is composed under the document camera as children come up to write the missing high-frequency words. As we write together, I am careful to coach into sentences that lend themselves to a number of known high-frequency words. The letter is then copied and sent home for children to share with families.

Self-Talk Posters

While creating self-talk posters for our mindset work, children begin making their own lines to anchor words. After coming up with the text, we count the words, and then the child draws the corresponding number of lines on their chart. For students who need it, these lines become a strategy for remembering the number of words in a sentence and leaving spaces in their independent writing.

UMazD

SGARD

USLEKP

Feeling Words

By November, students work to stretch longer, more complex words and write all the sounds they hear. Creating a poster about feelings, they tackle blends (sg for sc in scared) and make sure every word has at least one vowel. And because I want them to have plenty of time to explore and play with the skills and strategies they're learning in more structured interactive writing sessions, I stand back, out of their way, while they create this poster mostly on their own. My job here is to be a cheerleader, gently nudge them to write more sounds, and simply praise their efforts. This is their project and whatever spelling approximations they use I celebrate!

Whole-group interactive writing usually takes place on the carpet in the regular meeting area. Every child should be able to see the piece being composed, and there should be room for students to stand near the easel to write. Try to position yourself next to the easel. If possible, either kneel on the floor or sit in a chair. Body language is powerful. Whenever possible, remaining on approximately the same level as your students sends a message.

Principles of Interactive Writing

As teaching tools go, interactive writing is fairly simple and straightforward, but the more you understand about the principles behind the practice, the more effectively you can use the tool to support your students. Let's think now about some key principles. Interactive writing:

* is a *community experience*
* gives writers a safe place to explore *risk-taking*
* provides children *scaffolding* in the writing process
* is *differentiated*
* is *flexible* and *responsive*
* *happens often.*

Interactive Writing Is a Community Experience

When students walk into my classroom on the first day of school, it is a sparse place. Not much is up on the walls in the way of decorations or displays. There aren't giant colorful exhibitions of welcome that took me weeks to create. And contrary to what you might think, the children don't seem to mind. *We are starting kindergarten! We are simply excited to be at school!*

The mostly empty classroom sends an important message: "This space is ours and it is ready for us to make it our own—not only with our bodies and minds, but with our important work. I've been waiting . . . and you are finally here! Now the exciting work of building our community begins!"

Over the next few weeks, the walls begin to fill with the artifacts of our learning, and many of them we create during interactive writing. Children learn quickly through the routines of interactive writing that it is a community process, a time when we all work *together* to create and then use text. And in addition to the rich teaching of content taking place during interactive writing, children come to understand the power of working together toward a common goal and how our voices together are stronger than alone.

Now you may be wondering—if only one child is working at the easel with the teacher at a time, how is this a *community* activity? What are the rest of the students doing? Good questions! You may have noticed in the opening scene that I continually and explicitly invite the other children to help the student and me as we're writing. My main goal is to have their *thinking* engaged as we work together, but I also often invite them to *physically* engage by doing things such as:

There is a difference between decoration and display. For generations, teachers have "decorated" classrooms, using seasonal materials and other colorful items to make the space look pleasant and inviting. But we have learned that it is more important to fill the walls with work that is created by the children themselves. (McCarrier, Fountas, and Pinnell 2000)

Writing in the Air

Writing on the Floor with a Finger

Writing in Their Hand

Writing on the Back of the Child in Front of Them

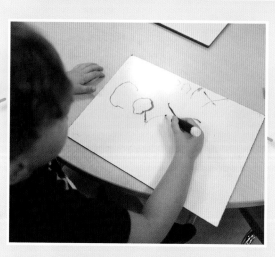

Writing on a Whiteboard with a Marker

Writing on Paper on a Clipboard with a Pencil

In addition to anchor charts, you can use interactive writing to document all kinds of things. The list below is certainly not exhaustive—the sky's the limit!

VIDEO 1.4: *What Are the Rest of the Kids Doing? Engaging Kids Physically*

Shared Experiences

Field trips

Assemblies

Guest speakers

Content-specific inquiry

Bulletin boards

Nature walks or city walks

Unique happenings (a bird's nest found on the playground, a spider that won't leave the classroom, etc.)

Shared Needs

Class rules

Daily schedule

Calendar items

Expectations for work times

Word walls

Color words, number words, etc.

Procedures for almost anything (arriving at school, using the bathroom, etc.)

Helpful labels

> [C]hildren are moving from an idea in the mind to its expression as words on paper. But this is not one act; it is many acts. A beginning writer may not be able to focus on all of these at once. As the child's focus and effort shift, so can the adult's response, repeating the child's words—holding on to them so she doesn't forget them as she goes through the physical act of writing—nudging toward the forging of letter/sound connections, appreciating the child's product, and so on.
>
> (Lindfors 2008)

Interactive Writing Gives Writers a Safe Space to Explore Risk-Taking

The relationships we build with children starting on those warm end-of-summer days help foster a community where they feel ready to do new and hard things. When our students know they are cared for and safe, they are more willing to trust us with challenges presented, and make no mistake about it, writing can feel like quite a challenge to a beginner.

Consider, for example, everything a beginning writer must do to write a simple sentence like the one below.

Instead of focusing on what the child doesn't yet know when you look at this sentence, think instead about what it would take to write this sentence independently. A writer would have to:

* have the idea in the flow of whatever they are writing
* think of the words for the idea—say them
* say them again to solidify, make sure they stay the same
* isolate the first word—requires one-to-one match
* say the word slowly
* isolate the first sound they hear
* identify which letter goes with the sound
* think about what that letter looks like and form it
* say the word slowly again
* if they hear another sound, identify which letter goes with it
* think about what that letter looks like and form it
* say the word again slowly . . . repeat until they think they have all the sounds
* say the sentence they wanted to write again
* isolate the next word
* remember to make a space
* say the word slowly
* isolate the first sound they hear
* identify which letter goes with that sound
* think about what that letter looks like and form it
* continue this process to capture every letter for every word—without forgetting what they were trying to write in the first place!

(See Matt Glover's video on YouTube about supporting spelling at home [Glover 2020].)

VIDEO 1.5: *Creating a Safety Net*

What a challenge! We ask children to take a lot of *new* information—letter names, sounds, writing pathways, conventions of writing—and orchestrate it all into a piece of text. For many, simply getting started putting pencil to paper is tricky. They worry about making it "right"—did I spell this correctly? Does this say *I love you Mom*? Left unchecked, the worries can overtake the writing. Part of our job as teachers is to help children understand that writing is a process—a messy one—that *all* writers partake in. The first step is getting started.

Interactive writing allows us to introduce children to the process of writing and all its intricacies in a safe, structured, manner. We effectively create a safety net for students to participate in the writing process. We guide them, sometimes literally by taking their hand, through the beginning steps of taking pen to paper and creating text. The goal is for the scaffolds we offer in this daily routine to transfer to children's independent writing, where the risks may feel even greater.

The Risk	How Interactive Writing Helps
What to write?	Through talking and planning, we decide on words and sentence structure. We plan how the words will look and fit on the page. We think through ways to come up with ideas.
What letters/sounds make up those words?	We work on being brave spellers together, saying words over and over slowly, stretching out words and sounds. We analyze letters, sounds, blends, digraphs, and all the skills we learn in phonics and how we can use them to make our words come alive on paper.
How do I form those letters?	We practice letter pathways together. We use hand-over-hand, tracing, and looking at direct models.
Spaces, punctuation, and capitalization, oh my! (All the conventions of writing)	We come up with many ways to leave spaces. We talk about all the different types of punctuation and how we decide to use them. We think out loud about when we need (and don't need) capital letters. We do all this together because we know it will make our writing easier to read.
What if I make a mistake?	We make mistakes. Lots of mistakes. We learn how to quickly cross off a mistake, fix it the best we can, and move on. We practice self-talk so mistakes don't cause our writing to stop.

How Interactive Writing Supports Risk-Taking

THREE WAYS TO UTILIZE INTERACTIVE WRITING

WHOLE GROUP

As we gather on the carpet, much like we do for a story or traditional lesson, the class is excited to help create an anchor chart or display. While only one child will come up at a time, we work together to help with all we know about letters, sounds, and words. When we collaborate, we are smarter, and our work shows it. What each child does when they come up looks different, as I tailor the experience to each child's skills and needs.

SMALL GROUP

Interactive writing is also a powerful tool to use with a small group of writers. While the whole group session will vary greatly depending on which writers are called up, in a small group the skills and strategies can be more focused and targeted toward the needs of the group. With fewer children to manage, we move quickly, allowing children to do more of the writing.

ONE-ON-ONE

With only one child, I can offer scaffolding and instruction right where it's needed most. Often with reluctant writers, this is a quick way to build confidence and get them writing. Many times, I will begin working with a child using interactive writing and, once the ball is rolling, leave them to work independently. "Look at all the writing we did together! Now you try it on your own! You can do it!"

VIDEO 1.6: *Interactive Writing in Small Groups*

A Teacher's Guide to Interactive Writing

Interactive Writing Provides Children with Scaffolding for the Writing Process

We've already thought about how challenging writing is for beginners, but as adults who've been writing for a long time, it can be easy to forget what this process is like. Sitting at my computer, my fingers must know which keys to hit to string letters together to form words, and when I write on paper, my hand "remembers" how to hold the pen and the pathways to form each letter. So many of the complexities involved in the transcription process of writing (getting the words down) become second nature to us the more we do it. Like riding a bike, once we know how to do it, we can simply hop on and our body seemingly takes over.

For our youngest writers, the challenge of transcription can feel insurmountable. In interactive writing, we provide instructional scaffolds (Vygotsky 1978) as we walk children through these tricky tasks, little by little showing them how to orchestrate all the skills into a piece of writing—something they'll then go do on their own, as best they can, from the very first days of school. And just like the scaffolding erected around buildings during construction, the support of interactive writing is meant to be temporary—a tool to help with the job. We don't want or intend to leave it up forever.

Interactive writing is chock full of scaffolds to help make the difficult task of writing more accessible for children. For example, just consider all the different scaffolds I might use to help children make a chart about their experience carving a pumpkin.

TIP!

Promote transfer and independence by being transparent with children about the scaffolds you use. For example, you might say something like, "These lines help us as we're learning to remember the words in our sentences and to leave spaces, but we won't always use them. They're like the training wheels on your bike—eventually, you want to stop using them."

[I]t involves a kind of "scaffolding" process that enables a child or novice to solve a problem, carry out a task or achieve a goal which would be beyond his unassisted efforts.

(Wood, Brunner, and Ross 1976)

SCAFFOLDING THE WRITING PROCESS

Skill/Idea

What words will convey the ideas?

Scaffold

* Student conversation with teacher guidance to support particular skills
* Partner conversations

What it Might Sound Like

"What was the first thing we did before carving? Turn and talk to your partner. The first thing we did was . . ."

Skill/Idea

Print carries meaning, goes from left to right, and then return sweeps.

Scaffold

Together we think of an idea, choose the words, and record those words on paper.

What it Might Sound Like

"Watch me write 'How to Carve a Pumpkin' across the top of our paper. When I get to the end of the line, I move my marker down and start at the beginning of the next line."

How to Carve a Pumpkin

1. mak a PLN !

2. Dro it on the PAPR.

3. Draw it on the PUMPKID.

4. KUt the TOP oFF.

5. skoop it oWt.

6 CRV it

Skill/Idea

Which letter/sound do we record?

Scaffold

* Name a letter and its associated sound(s).
* Model how to use the alphabet chart as a tool.

What it Might Sound Like

"The word 'make' has three sounds: /m/ /a/ /k/. Let's start with /m/. What do you hear? Yes, the letter M makes the /m/ sound—write it!"

Skill/Idea

What punctuation is needed at the end of a sentence?

Scaffold

* Teach punctuation marks explicitly.
* Record the punctuation when pre-planning a sentence with lines for words.

What it Might Sound Like

"'Plan' is the last word in the sentence, and we're really excited about making a plan. Let's put an exclamation point here so the reader knows."

Skill/Idea

Knowing certain words can help us read and write many others.

Scaffold

* Teacher voices over word-family power. ("If I know 'in', I can write 'fin'.")
* Teacher models how to use the word wall.

What it Might Sound Like

"Yes, the word 'in' is on our word wall. How do you spell 'in'?"

A Teacher's Guide to Interactive Writing

Skill/Idea

How do we write/form letters?

Scaffold

* ✳ Models and voice-letter pathways
* ✳ Hand-over-hand
* ✳ Trace with yellow marker/highlighter

What it Might Sound Like

"M starts with a big line down, then another big line down, up, and finally one last big line down."

Skill/Idea

What is the difference between letters and words?

Scaffold

Discuss letters/sounds and show how they come together to create words.

What it Might Sound Like

"'Cut' is the first word. Let's say it slowly. There are three sounds—/c/ /u/ /t/—and three letters in the word 'cut.' What's first?"

Skill/Idea

Words need spaces between them.

Scaffold

* ✳ Make lines for words with spaces between them.
* ✳ Use fingers to create a space between words.

What it Might Sound Like

"Let's put a finger up each time we say a word. Yes, five words, so I'll draw five lines with a space in between each one."

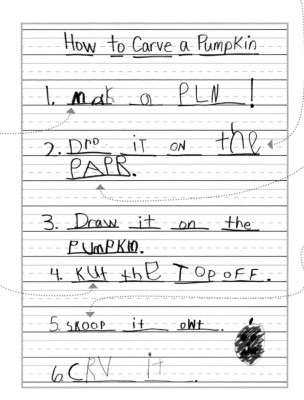

Skill/Idea

Knowing the letters/sounds in a word

Scaffold

Say the word slowly, repeating until all sounds heard are recorded.

What it Might Sound Like

"'Paper'—what do you hear at the beginning? Yes, /p/. Write it! Now say the word again, slowly, with me—paaaper. What's next?"

Skill/Idea

Letters can work together in different ways.

Scaffold

Explicit instruction about digraphs/blends, voicing over and modeling how to use them

What it Might Sound Like

"'Scoop'—what do you hear at the beginning? Yes, S, and a /c/ sound right after. Those two sounds together sound like /sk/. What will you write?"

VIDEO 1.7: *Differentiation in Interactive Writing*

Scaffolds depend on understanding a child's Zone of Proximal Development, "It is the distance between the actual developmental level as determined by independent problem solving and the level of potential development as determined through problem-solving under adult guidance, or in collaboration with more capable peers."

(Vygotsky 1978)

Interactive Writing Is Differentiated

While we may decide to focus on a particular skill during an interactive writing session, there is a wide range of skills and strategies we can cover to meet the needs of diverse learners in a single setting. Students with IEPs or emergent bilinguals—all children can feel successful when we help them access writing at their instructional levels.

Interactive writing provides multiple levels of scaffolding and asks students to take agency for what level they need right now. Generally speaking, with our youngest writers in pre-K, we'll provide the highest levels of scaffolding and then slowly taper it as our students learn and grow. We ask children to think about the question "What do I need right now to help me do this?" and then we offer them that support. When this question becomes a habit of mind, it helps children take responsibility for their learning and transfer the content to independent writing.

On page 23, you'll see two skills—spaces between words and what letter do I write. We might be working on them as a whole class, but the teaching can be differentiated for each student who is asked to come up and share the pen.

Interactive writing allows us to tailor our instruction to the individual child we call up to share the pen while the rest of the class listens, observes, and participates from the rug as we voice over other options or offer thinking at various levels. If we teach children to respect different learning styles and speeds, they almost always will honor their classmates. We also keep them engaged by empowering them to be teachers and helpers to their classmates.

SPACES BETWEEN WORDS

Teacher draws lines for words.

Student draws lines for words.

Student uses finger after each word to create space.

Student slides or jumps hand after each word.

WHAT LETTER DO I WRITE?

Teacher makes the sound and helps child identify corresponding letter on alphabet chart.

Teacher makes sound, child replicates sound, and they work together to identify corresponding letter on alphabet chart.

Child makes sound and works with teacher or classmates to identify corresponding letter on alphabet chart.

Child makes sound and identifies letter independently.

PLASTIC

PAPER

TIPS FOR PRE-K:
THE REASONS TO START INTERACTIVE WRITING IN PRESCHOOL ABOUND

* It allows your students to see themselves as writers.
* It invites them into the writing process.
* It is engaging and FUN.
* It is a community experience.

TIP!

1 Teacher led—Many teachers feel that students need to be doing all of the writing when we invite them up. NOT SO! Interactive writing means we write **together.** For most preschool interactive writing, the children will only be writing a single letter. I'd start with inviting no more than three to four children up per session. You will be writing most of the text.

4 What are the other children doing?—When you invite individual students up, you need the other children to be engaged. First, start by setting expectations. Let them know, "We all have to help Lily write this sound—let's make sure we help her!" This reinforces the community aspect of interactive writing. I always give the class a 'job' to do. With preschool aged children, it's typically writing the letter in the air with their finger. This promotes gross motor movement and also allows you to informally assess their grasp of writing the letter. You can also provide whiteboards and markers or paper and pencils on clipboards and ask them to write the letters.

2 Keep it short—When starting, keep it short. Like really short. Maybe a single sentence. And keep that sentence short! No more than four or five words to start. This way, you can count the words with children—put a finger up for each word. As you do this work, you're talking about concepts about print—words vs. letters—oh, and you're counting together too! Once your students are used to the routine and have some practice, you can write slightly longer sentences. Next, you'll move to two sentences. Build up slowly—this isn't a race! You can also invite children to help you create charts and labels for the classroom.

3 Hand-over-hand—If your students aren't writing any letters independently yet, invite them up anyway! With the child's consent, offering hand-over-hand, you can guide them, and they'll feel supported and confident. I typically start with the first letter in a child's name. Once they can write this, move on to other letters in their name. If we're writing the sentence "I like peanut butter," I will invite Lily, Paul, and Brian to write the L, P, and B. If there are no students whose names start with those letters, I'll look for other letters in their names.

5 Celebrate!—I always say my number one job as a writing teacher is being a cheerleader. Celebrate every effort. Celebrate every piece. Once you've worked together to write 'I like peanut butter,' let the children draw and color the paper during snack or choice time. Put it up. Make it a bulletin board. Snap a photo on your phone and share it with families.

Interactive Writing Is Flexible and Responsive

One of the aspects of interactive writing I love most (and what can make it so tricky) is how unpredictable it can be. Let's face it: working with small children, you never know what might happen. You can plan for days and days, but once that plan is in motion, you get what you get.

For this reason, I like to approach interactive writing with a "here's what I hope happens" mentality. By definition, a plan is a proposal for doing something and that's exactly my intent—an invitation to my class and the universe for things to go a certain way.

Figuring out "what the child is trying to do" at a given moment is not easy. Often, we get it wrong. But our chances of getting it right are never better than in one-on-one collaborative writing events. This child, this moment, this literate act: this supportive partnership.

(Lindfors 2008)

LANGUAGE THAT SUPPORTS A RANGE OF LEARNING STYLES AND SPEEDS

Evan, I know you know how to spell "because" so keep that in your brain and let Tim do his best thinking work—but pay attention because we may need your help!

Everyone say "walk." Now say it again slowly. Think, "What sounds do I hear?" Now keep those letters in your brain as Lucy writes the word with me. She may ask someone for help!

Hmm, /ing/—does anyone know how to spell /ing/? I feel like there are some friends who might know this.

Ultimately, regardless of how much thinking I do about an interactive writing session, what actually happens often surprises me. Sometimes it's a wonderful surprise, and sometimes not, but either way I have to be flexible and responsive in the teaching moment.

Here's an example. Writing came easily to Naomi. By January, she knew all her letter sounds and was writing long, complicated words using developmental spelling, but she wasn't leaving spaces between her words.

When I invited Naomi up to work on the chart, I did plan to teach into leaving spaces, but I wanted to be flexible and responsive to Naomi's intentions at the same time.

▶ **Me:** Naomi, let's make a plan for leaving spaces. Should we draw lines, or do you want to use your finger to leave room?

Naomi: Neither. I actually have a new way to leave spaces.

▶ **Me:** What? A new way? What is it? Tell us!

▲ **Naomi:** After I write a word, I just slide my hand over.

▶ **Me:** Ok, let's watch Naomi write "we" and then see how her hand slides over.

▶ **Me:** Wait, did you see it? Thumbs up if you saw it. Now, did you hear it? I actually heard Naomi's hand slide across the paper as she left space! Did you? Thumbs up if you could hear it. Naomi is going to write the next word. Now let's watch and listen for "the slide."

Naomi surprised me. She had been drawing lines for her words until right before she explained her new strategy in front of the whole class, so I wasn't expecting this development. In the midst of my teaching, I had to listen, be responsive, and pivot when Naomi told me she had a new idea. In the next chapter, I'll share some essential teaching moves you can use to help you respond to common scenarios you'll likely encounter during interactive writing.

I'm voicing over the idea of making a plan. This is something we're all working on and so we need to be thinking about spaces before we even begin writing.

I'm being dramatic here for effect, but I am genuinely intrigued and curious.

This is the goal of all our spacing work—simply sliding your hand over after each word—something experienced writers don't even think about. Naomi has named it.

She writes we as the class watches intently, and in the silence as they stare, we can actually hear her hand slide across the paper.

I name her move 'the slide' and it becomes part of our repertoire of strategies for leaving a space. Children are intrigued and excited about a new strategy and many try it both when they come up for interactive writing and during independent writing.

The handwritten chart reads:

Armadillos

Body
- As Big As A Cat
- Small head
- Long snout
- Carapace - thick outer skin

Habitat
- They dig burrows.
- Can live in logs
- grasslands and forests

Food/Prey
- Omnivor
- mostly eat beetles
- ants, termites, spiders, berries, roots

Predators
- Joguars
- snakes
- coyotes
- bears

Facts
- Nocturnal
- hold their breath for 6 minutes
- sixty insects at once
- the babes are cold pups
- 21 types
- 2 roll into a ball

Most writers go through a developmental stage where they are learning to space, and it's something I often teach into during interactive writing—drawing lines for words to emphasize spacing and/or using our fingers to leave a space after each word. This chart about armadillos shows a variety of ways writers, including Naomi, planned for spacing.

About Bees

- Bees hav 5 eyes
- Bees hav 4 Wines
- Bees are Hairy
- Bees Have Baskets for POllen
- BeeS HAV A LonG Tounge for DrinKing NECtAr
- Bees Dance to Give Pirections

After spotting several bees on the playground (and having various reactions to them), we decided to go to the library and check out some nonfiction books about bees. As we studied them, we took notes to document and share our learning.

Interactive Writing *Happens Often*

Like anything we want children to internalize, we have to provide thoughtful and frequent practice. At the beginning of the school year, it helps to look at your schedule and think about small chunks of time when you can gather children for interactive writing. Sometimes before specials such as Art, Music, or Library, or when you return from recess, or when you've got a few minutes before packing up to go home, you can write together. Then as you move through the year, think about the content you're teaching and how you can utilize interactive writing to enhance your lessons. When you make interactive writing a priority, it happens often.

You will also find lots of opportunities for interactive writing if you simply listen to your students not only during lessons but when they arrive and when they are eating snack or playing at recess. Get to know their interests and what they're curious about and look for opportunities to invite them up to write with you. When you create an environment rich in student writing, children will ask to write and create text together.

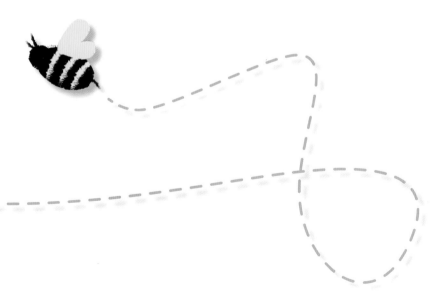

In my classroom, most whole-group interactive writing sessions last ten to fifteen minutes. When planning, it helps to remember that children do best when we ask them to sit for only the number of minutes equivalent to their age, so asking five-, six-, and seven-year-olds to sit much longer than ten minutes is an exercise in frustration for everyone. Also, I find that writing in smaller amounts of time helps build my students' stamina and makes it likely I will fit interactive writing in more often.

VIDEO 1.8: *Opportunities for Interactive Writing*

Typical Timing for an Interactive Writing Session

2–3 minutes
Teacher sets the purpose for the interactive writing and basic planning takes place.

8–10 minutes
Teacher and students compose and write the piece together.

2–3 minutes
Teacher leads students in reviewing/revising/reading piece together.

A few students asked if we could create a chart of math choices for them. Working in a small group, we created this list to display.

Simple charts can be completed in a single session, but often we work over the course of a few days to a week to complete more complicated charts, stories, or letters. When interactive writing stretches over several days, it helps children understand that the writing process isn't something that often happens in one sitting—on the contrary, that rarely happens! And, of course, working on writing over time is a process we'll ask students to replicate during their independent writing. To help children understand the temporal nature of process, I might use language that sounds like the examples below at the beginning and end of several interactive writing sessions where we are working on a single text.

LANGUAGE TO ENCOURAGE PROCESS

Day/Session 1

Beginning
"Today we'll start writing a piece."

End
"Tomorrow/later today we'll continue working on this."

Day/Session 2

Beginning
"Yesterday we started working on ... Let's review what we wrote and keep going!"

End
"We're still not finished but look at all we've done! Let's read it together and plan what we'll work on next time."

Day/Session 3

Beginning
"Wow, look at how hard we've worked so far. First we ... Next we ..."

End
"Let's finish our piece together!"

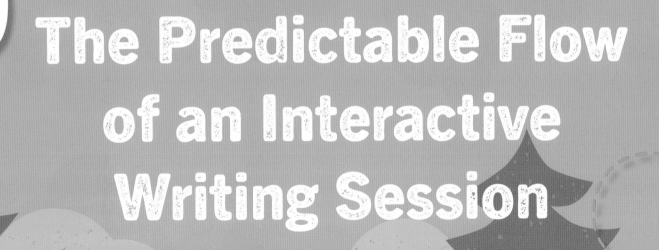

The Predictable Flow of an Interactive Writing Session

Interactive writing is, at its heart, a collaborative and interactive experience. As you work to understand this approach to teaching, which delves deep into the writing process, you and your students inevitably have rich conversations about writing.

(Roth and Dabrowski 2016)

WHILE EVERY INTERACTIVE WRITING SESSION IS FLUID, RESPONSIVE, and malleable, most lessons have the same key components that basically mirror the writing process.

As a teaching structure, interactive writing is designed so that at every stage of the session, you will find opportunities to teach children—in a highly scaffolded manner—about the writing process that they can use on their own during independent writing. Let's explore each of those opportunities a little more now.

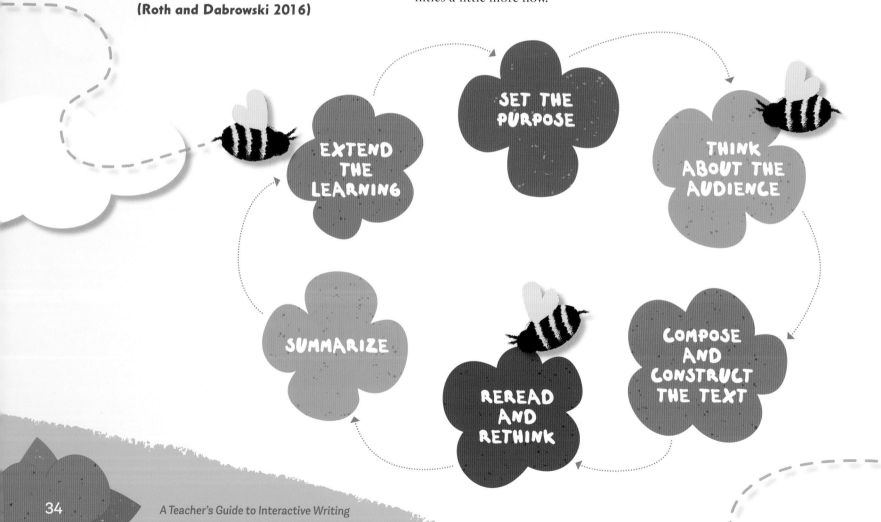

SET THE PURPOSE

THINK ABOUT THE AUDIENCE

EXTEND THE LEARNING

COMPOSE AND CONSTRUCT THE TEXT

SUMMARIZE

REREAD AND RETHINK

Set the Purpose

The first thing writers must do is come up with an idea, and that's where you will start with interactive writing, too. Arguably, the blank page is the most challenging aspect of writing. It's what sometimes leads children to sit and do anything but write during writing workshop. It's what often convinces teachers to give children writing prompts instead of teaching them how to find their own ideas. But with interactive writing, you can show children again and again how good ideas for writing are all around them! While interactive writing is meant to support what children do independently during writing time, the teaching practice itself doesn't have to be connected to writing time at all. A day of learning with children is filled with great reasons to pick up a pen and write. When interactive writing is used purposefully across the day, children see the why behind the writing and learn so much about what compels people to write.

At first, you will probably have to lead the way, offering up ideas for interactive writing, but every time you gather to create a new piece, you are planting a seed, showing children that writing is a way to hold onto ideas they want to share or remember. As you experience stories, new learning, and events, children learn that documenting these together is an important function of their community. Over time, as your students see the many purposes writing can fulfill, they will almost certainly begin leading the way and suggesting "Let's make a sign!" or "We can make a chart!"

One of the most beautiful aspects of interactive writing is that you need so little to do it. An easel. Some chart paper. A marker. You're ready to go! Other items are nice to have, but they're certainly not required.

INTERACTIVE WRITING ESSENTIALS

Basics	Optional
Easel	Different-colored markers
Chart Paper	Correction tape
Marker	Highlighter (for tracing)
	Sentence Strips
	Whiteboards, markers, erasers for students
	Clipboards, paper, pencils for students

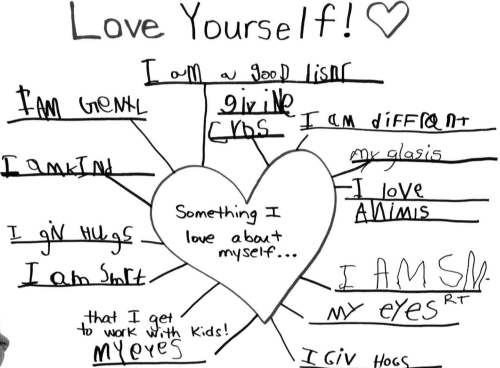

Love Yourself! ♡

I am a good lisnr

I AM GrenL

givine crbs

I am diffrqnt

my glasis

I am kINd

I love ANimis

I giv HUgs

Something I love about myself...

I am Smrt

I AM SN

that I get to work with kids!

MY eyes RT

MY eyes

I giv Hogs

After talking about the word *love* at Valentine's Day, we made a quick chart of all the reasons to love yourself. I made this chart entirely with my students, drawing the lines for each phrase, the heart in the middle, and explaining how the diagram worked as I drew. After a short discussion and some thinking time, each child came up to share and write a short phrase using high-frequency words.

Responding to Literature

When readers read, they think, they feel, they wonder—and sometimes they capture all of this reflection with writing. After reading, you can use interactive writing to capture your students' responses to a text (the way older students might use a journal for this same purpose).

Resilient – WEn you hAV TRuBul , you BOWNS bac !

While studying the mindset stances from *Mindset for Learning* (Mraz and Hertz 2015), we read *Oh No, George!* by Chris Naughton and made a chart for the new vocabulary word *resilient*.

happy ☺	sad ☹	mad/angry ☹
Cheerful	diSappointed	
Excited	Devastated	Frustrated
Thrilled	Whiny	Upset
Ecstatic	Weepy	Furious
Joyful		Grumpy
		Annoyed

As part of our push to use more precise vocabulary when talking about characters in books, we crafted this chart together. We had been talking about this work for some time and a student suggested, "Maybe we need a chart to help us remember."

After reading a nonfiction leveled reader about basketball, a girl in the small group asked me, "Mr. Halpern, why are there no girls in this book?" I didn't have a good answer. Another child replied, "Why don't we fix it?" I grabbed some large sticky notes, scissors, and a pen, and we fixed it. We changed *boys* to *children* and added photos representing a variety of gender expressions.

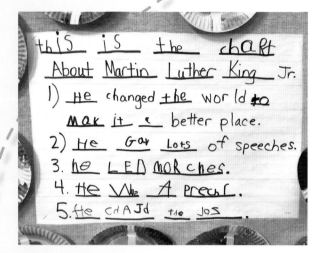

After studying Dr. King and the Civil Rights Movement for several weeks, the class wanted to document our learning with a chart to display. Children brainstormed important facts to remember and then came up to help write. I shared the load by writing for them "About Martin Luther King, Jr." in the title (" 'About'—that's a tricky word, here's how you write it.") and all of the words not underlined in the chart. This saved time and kept the pace moving quickly to keep engagement up as we worked.

Content-Area Study

When teaching subject-area content, you often need charts, graphs, tables, etc., to help illustrate and reinforce learning. Instead of buying or creating them on your own, you can use interactive writing and let your students participate in the process. Their learning is more likely to stick, and you'll be able to layer in literacy skills on top of the subject-area content.

During math time, a small group of first graders (who are more independent than pre-K and kindergarten students) created the days and months on this calendar. As they worked, I coached into their approximations, reinforcing correct spelling since we'd also be using the calendar to learn to spell the days of the week. Children then added numbers each day during the calendar portion of our math workshop. Some teachers have students add numbers and do any writing ahead of time (during arrival, snack time, etc.) and then review the calendar with the whole group.

Created while studying word families, we worked together to make a chart to help us remember and review in future lessons and for students to use during independent writing.

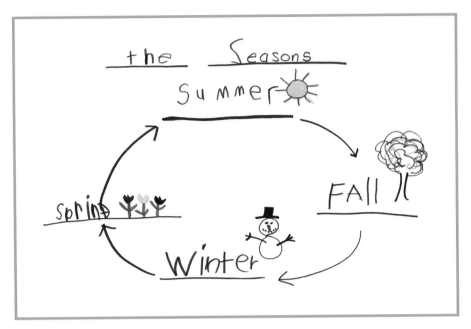

During our study of weather, we created a simple flow chart showing the seasons. Children came up and did the writing and we discussed what pictures might go with each. Then during Choice Time, I invited students over to add illustrations.

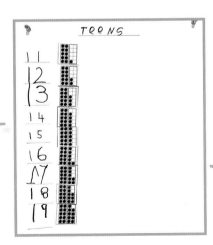

As we started to study numbers in the teens, we needed a chart to show the different ways to represent each number. The students wrote the title and all the numbers, and we added a little to it each day as we studied the numbers.

Interactive writing helps build a bridge between writing and all other areas of the curriculum.

(Patterson, Schaller, and Clemens 2008)

During a week-long inquiry into penguins, we learned that sometimes readers take notes to help them remember important facts they learn. This chart was created over the course of the week, and we added to it after each book we read. We then labeled a picture of a penguin I traced from one of our books

In kindergarten, I like to teach children what active listening looks and feels like, and then give them time to practice. We do this by making a chart together.

Procedures, Routines, and Expectations

Think about all the things you put in place to make your days with students run smoothly. Your community's procedures, routines, and expectations form some of the most important content you teach. With interactive writing, you can bring students into the process not just of recording this content, but also thinking through—as a community—what it should be.

We worked together to create this chart to help students solve their own problems. We first brainstormed ways to solve a problem, and I took photos of children acting out each scenario. Children then worked in pairs, using the photographs to help them write. We then gathered as a class to assemble and read the chart.

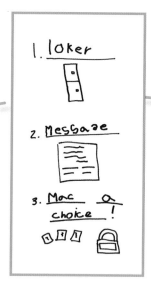

Helping children with the arrival routine can be tricky. I love to stand in the door and hallway greeting and chatting with students as they arrive, but I also need to manage them as they enter the classroom and begin their days. One way to help is by making a chart for students to use as they enter the classroom. I made this short list with two students who needed support in this area. Then we shared it with the entire class before hanging it up near the door.

Community Experiences

Interactive writing is itself a community effort, so using it to build and expand your time as a community should feel quite natural. Any time you gather and share a common experience, writing together about it can be part of that process.

The helper for the day wrote some missing high-frequency words with me. The class helped her as needed.

I drew a simple happy face and a sad face. A student added a line through the circled faces to remind us to use more precise language during reading workshop.

We added a simple reminder about How-To writing during writing workshop.

This cluster of seven smiley faces and a table were drawn while solving number stories during math time.

[At the bottom] Children each wrote the new high-frequency word " was" after reading the message.

Good Morning!

Today is Tuesday.

We ⁱHaV P.E. and Music

Evie is the HeLPer.

Love, how to

Mr Halpern

Write was

How to
1 In order
2 steps

Write was

Each morning, children walk into the classroom and know that part of their job is to read the morning message. They gather, helping each other decode, and then add something to the bottom (write a high-frequency word, answer a math problem, draw a shape, etc.). I write the message on paper and keep it up all day so we can interact with it or add to it whenever it makes sense. I prefer using paper over dry erase because paper can document so much of our learning throughout the day and allows us to revisit and reflect before heading home. If I need a fresh sheet for something, I swing the old one over, but I don't rip the morning message off until the day is over.

Special Events

Documenting life is part of writing. When something special happens, we take pictures, we reminisce, we write.

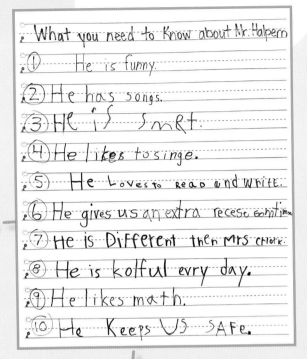

What you need to Know about Mr. Halpern

① He is funny.

② He has songs.

③ He is smrt.

④ He likes to singe.

⑤ He Loves to Read and write.

⑥ He gives us an extra recese somtimx

⑦ He is Different then Mrs chork.

⑧ He is kolful evry day.

⑨ He likes math.

⑩ He Keeps US SAFe.

One school year, when I took over a first-grade class unexpectedly, I was asked to have an open house midyear. After spending a few weeks getting to know the children, we made a chart together to help them share a little about me with their families. "Your families are coming to meet me and see our classroom. What do you think are the most important things for them to know about me?"

TIP!

Asking your students inquiry-based questions is a good way to get them thinking about ideas for interactive writing.

❋ "What have we learned about . . . ?"

❋ "How can we share/show our learning?"

❋ "What are the most important parts? What do we need to make sure we write?"

❋ "Do you have any ideas about how we can organize our piece?"

❋ "Is there another/better way to show this?"

IT's great to be

dIFFERENT

• curly hair
• gIAS IS

• twins
• SKin KULR
  TAll
• SHORT
• Frecls
• FAMIlEZ

When I saw this unique stuffy at a local craft fair, I figured he deserved a home in my classroom. When I introduced him to my class, they first decided to name him "Mr. Happy Pants" and then asked why I picked him from all those available. When I told them, "He's different and we've been talking about differences," they suggested, "Let's make a chart about all the ways it's great to be different!"

Think About the Audience

The audience for writing—who will read it and needs to understand it—is almost always tied to the purpose for writing. And while there are so many reasons you will find to write with your students, you really only need to keep two potential audiences in mind for interactive writing:

YOUR CLASS	NOT YOUR CLASS
Children and adults in your classroom.	Children and adults not in your classroom. This might include other teachers and staff, other students in the school, parents and families, community members, etc.

With this simple distinction, you can teach children a lot about how writers consider audience and purpose as they compose. Audience and purpose, of course, determine how much revision and editing writers do and what the final piece will look like. As you consider each piece of interactive writing you create with your students, you can include them in the process of thinking about the audience.

Here are some different ways that might sound:

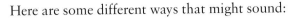

* "We're going to make a chart to help us remember names of shapes. Since this is just for us, we'll simply do our best spelling and make sure we can read it."

* "This letter is a welcome to our families. Because we're sharing this with them, I'll help you make sure everything looks great for them."

* "We're adding some text to a book we read that we want to share with friends outside our class. Do you think we need to make sure everything is spelled correctly before we finish?"

* "This sign is staying in our room. It's to help us remember when it's ok to interrupt me. Talk to your partner about how you think it needs to look."

When you make the thinking about audience explicit, you boost the transfer of this skill to independent writing and help children understand why it's okay if their finished writing isn't always perfect. Ultimately, you want children to feel free to write, write, write, and the more leeway you give them around spelling and conventions, the more they will write. And the more they write, the more you can teach into spelling and conventions.

VIDEO 2.1: *Developmental vs. Conventional Spelling*

Developmental vs. Conventional Spelling

Developmental spelling (also called approximated spelling or invented spelling) is the type of spelling young writers use when they are learning to spell. As children begin to understand the relationships between letters and sounds, spelling patterns, and conventions, they begin to write words in a way that makes perfect sense to them (but not as much to adults without years of experience reading developmental spelling).

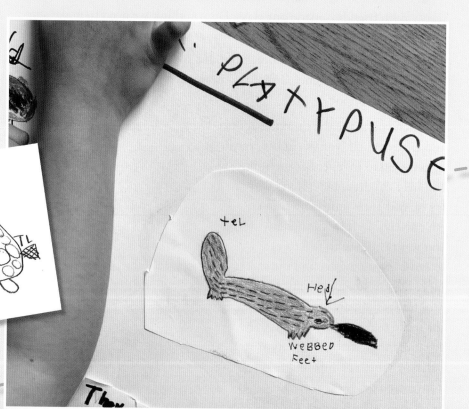

Examples of Children's Developmental Spelling

> **Writing needs to be a friend, and it needs to be a tool. And that's what my job is; to help them know this.**
>
> (Lindfors 2008)

The conventional spelling of a word is the one found in the dictionary, and it takes into account hundreds of rules about spelling that often don't make sense from a simple letter-sound perspective. Oh, and those hundreds of rules all have various exceptions. For example, when you think about a word like *perceive*, beyond the *P* at the beginning and the *V* near the end, the other letters don't really do what you'd think they should do. If I'm a beginning writer learning letters and sounds, I'd most likely write *perceive* as "prsev" and call it a day. Now, if I knew that every syllable must have at least one vowel, I might write, "persev" and think I was spot on.

You can see how conventional spelling is not something that's easy to figure out and why it takes years of reading and writing experience to become a good speller (and adults still give major props to dictionaries and spell-check).

Because the purpose of interactive writing is to offer a highly scaffolded instructional strategy to nudge budding writers to independence, generally I don't spell for children or correct their approximations unless the word or pattern is something I've explicitly taught and I know they're ready to take it on in this context. If I do nudge for a conventional spelling (or a closer-to-conventional spelling), I always connect back to purpose and make sure children know it's because we're writing for someone outside our classroom community.

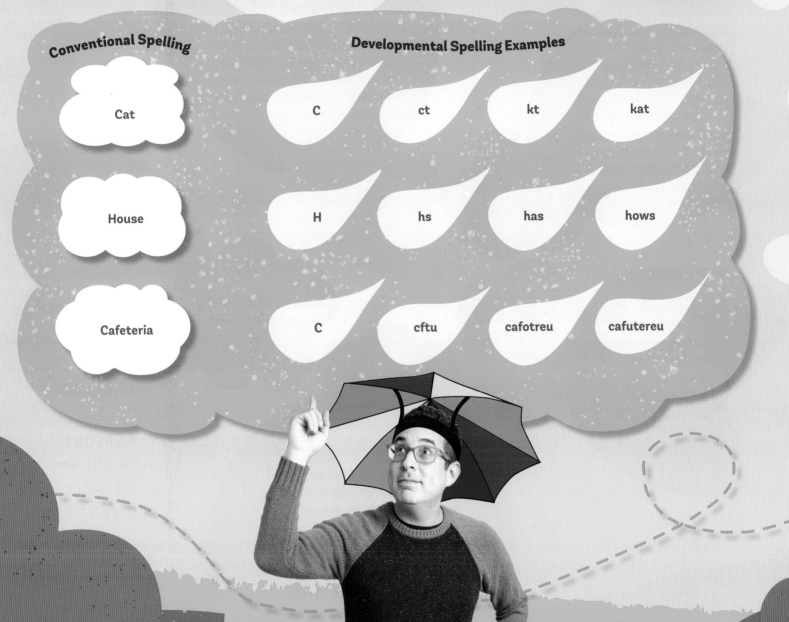

AS CHILDREN LEARN MORE, THEIR APPROXIMATIONS BECOME MORE SOPHISTICATED

Conventional Spelling

Developmental Spelling Examples

Cat

C   ct   kt   kat

House

H   hs   has   hows

Cafeteria

C   cftu   cafotreu   cafutereu

49

CONFIDENCE

When an adult always tells a child how to spell something correctly rather than teaching into how words work and supporting risk-taking, it sends a message about that child's ability to spell on their own, eroding the confidence they need for independent writing.

RISK-TAKING

Writing is risky, but when children are taught to value their smart, amazing approximations, they are more willing to risk spelling both simple and challenging words—something we need them to do over and over again.

INDEPENDENCE

Telling children how to spell a word (or correcting them) isn't teaching about spelling. To develop independence, children need us to teach them the ways letters work together, patterns, rules, exceptions, etc.— not spell for them.

LANGUAGE USAGE

If children feel comfortable writing only words they know how to spell, they'll be less likely to use more descriptive and interesting vocabulary.

RESEARCH

When children use developmental spelling, we are able to research what they know and then teach into the next step.

REASONS NOT TO SPELL FOR CHILDREN

Adapted from Matt Glover's video on YouTube "Supporting Spelling at Home" (Glover 2020)

Over time, as students' understandings about spelling grow through instruction and experience, you can hold them more accountable both in interactive and independent writing and nudge them toward more and more conventional spelling. Your nudges will look different for each child, of course, which is part of the power of interactive writing.

TIP!

When children approximate a spelling, they often will ask, "Is this right?" Responses like these celebrate their effort and encourage them to continue writing:

* "I see all the sounds in the word!"
* "Did you write all the sounds you heard?"
* "That looks good to me!"
* "Wow, you wrote so many sounds."
* "Let's read it and see if it looks right."

VIDEO 2.2: *Science of Reading and Interactive Writing*

[E]ach interactive writing lesson engage[s] students in the recursive processes of planning, drafting, revising, and editing of a group text.

(Williams 2018)

Compose and Construct the Text

Ah, now we get to the heart of it. Sitting by the easel, fresh paper and markers near, we are ready to write with our students. This is where the magic happens. This is where we take our students' hands and guide them through the journey of the writing process. Time and again we will say, "Remember how we did this together? Now you try it!" But first, we must write together.

When I'm planning an interactive writing session ahead of time, I do some basic setup work. Sometimes I'll add pictures or photos to the chart to save time, but sometimes I don't. Sometimes I'll cover those pictures and reveal them as we work, but sometimes I don't. Sometimes I'll jot down on a sticky note the basic idea of what I want parts of the chart to say, but sometimes I don't. And of course, sometimes we decide to do some writing together on the spur of the moment with no planning at all!

To help you understand some of the decision making that happens around interactive writing, let's consider two examples from my classroom—one where I did a lot of planning ahead and one that just happened organically.

An Example: Making a Management Chart for the Classroom

We were having a predictable problem in my classroom—children interrupting my reading conferences—so I decided we needed a tool to help address it. I planned and prepared a chart for interactive writing ahead of time, and then I brought the idea to my students:

Me: Readers, we have been doing such an amazing job with our independent reading! Remember, when you do your job, what am I able to do?

Class: Work with kids!

Me: That's right, I can sit and pull kids to help them with reading. But yesterday, when I was reading with Norah and Felix, something happened.

Norah chimes in: Yes! You kept stopping for things!

Me: Yes! Readers kept coming over and interrupting our work. How did you feel about that happening?

Norah: Well, we didn't get through the whole book. I didn't like that.

Felix: Yeah, I was bummed we didn't finish.

Me: Hmm, so I'm hearing that when other kids interrupt, we don't get to work as much. We don't get to read as much. And that is frustrating.

Norah and Felix: Yes!

Me: Hmm. Maybe we could create a chart to help all the kids in our class know when it's ok to interrupt me and when it's not. Do you think that's a good idea?

Class: Yes!

Notice that in this conversation, I've made sure that the purpose and audience for the writing are clear. We need to create a tool we can use in the classroom—a chart that lists the acceptable reasons to interrupt me when I'm working with students. Now, look closely at the chart and some of the teaching decisions and moves I made before and during the interactive writing session where we created it.

I had my students "turn and talk" about what we might call the chart as I listened in. Then I offered, "I heard so many ideas. How about if we call it 'When Can I Interrupt Mr. Halpern?'" I had made the lines for each word in this title ahead of time, and I had a different child come up to write each word. I wrote my name and the question mark to save time.

Each of these photographs was printed ahead of time, glued to the chart, and covered with a large sticky note. As I revealed each one, I'd say, "Turn and tell your partner what this could say." Then, to keep the pace brisk, I'd share out, "I heard 'fire'" or whatever I had preplanned for each line.

By January (when this chart was created), most writers understand CVC patterns. I knew we could tackle **fire** as three sounds and then I could offer the silent e on the end.

While the vowel in **lots** is incorrect, as we hadn't taken a deep dive into vowel sounds yet, and to keep the pace up, I didn't correct the child. I also looked at it as a future opportunity to edit.

Kermit is my cat and I write his name often in front of students, so many of them knew the correct spelling! Some words we simply know from using them often even if they aren't high-frequency words we've learned. Kermit's name was also a great opportunity to point out that every syllable has at least one vowel.

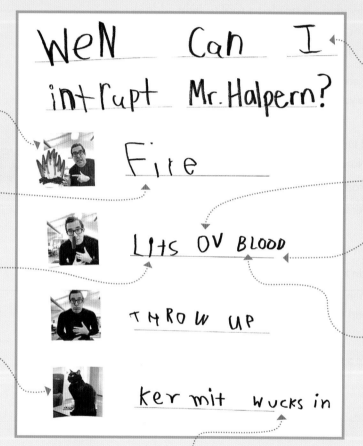

The title is simple, clear, and purposeful, and it includes the high-frequency words **can** and **I**.

I chose a different student to write each line based on the skill demands of each word and what I heard as they discussed their thinking.

Of was not a high-frequency word we knew, so I took the opportunity to teach into writing the sounds we hear when we don't know a word.

Here I had drawn a single line because I anticipated only writing **blood**. However, after discussing the picture, we decided **lots of blood** made more sense.

Blood is a tricky word, so we focused on the /bl/ blend and the final /d/ and I just supplied the vowels.

In is a high-frequency word we knew and that was on our word wall.

The child sounded out the word **walks**, and because the spelling is very close and made sense, I left it as is. To support brave spellers, I'm always looking for opportunities to reinforce "write what you hear" as a strategy.

As you plan for and compose interactive writing, think about what you are teaching in reading and writing. What have you learned and what are you about to learn? The goal is to create an interactive writing experience that:

* reinforces skills already taught
* plants seeds for future skills
* encourages risk-taking
* allows children to practice the transfer of phonics skills.

VIDEO 2.3: *Planning*

An Example: Welcoming Families to the Classroom

In the fall, as my students and I discussed the upcoming open house, we were inspired to write a letter to welcome families to our classroom (see Section One, page 8).

Me: Writers, tonight is our open house! It's so exciting! You'll be bringing your families to our school and classroom. What do you think you'll be doing when you come into our class?

Rebecca: Showing them stuff!

Hank: Showing them where we sit. And books! And maybe some play stuff.

Me: Yes! You'll get to show your families all the important parts of our room. Now, when you invite someone to a place that's new to them, it's sometimes nice to welcome them. Have you ever done anything to make someone feel welcome? Turn and talk to your partner about a time you made someone feel welcome. What did you do?

I listen for a bit and hear a variety of comments, but one catches my attention and gives me an idea:

Me: Yes! I heard some writers say, "You might put something out to welcome them!" What if we wrote a welcome note to our families? This way, when you bring them tonight, you can show them, read it with them, and they'll feel welcome. Do you think that's a good idea?

Class: Yes!

This note was made immediately in response to this conversation, so I didn't plan ahead for it. All the decisions about its composition and construction had to be in the moment. Let's look at some of them now.

To save time, I quickly wrote *This is our* [...]

I wrote the word *Good* and then selected a child who was working on reading and writing *-ing* (an advanced skill for September) to come up and write *EVENing*!

While we hadn't yet learned *we*, it is one of the first high-frequency words we do learn, so this was a good opportunity to teach into future learning.

Right out of the gate, I encourage children to "write what you hear," and the word *would* sounds exactly as this student wrote it. There are three sounds in the word and each sound is represented by a letter that makes sense.

This word was tricky. I knew one child, already a reader, might know the /sh/ blend so I selected him. Then I told him to write the *ow* for the long *o* sound at the end.

While *the* is a high-frequency word we'd learn shortly, I chose to write it to help keep the session short. I voiced over my actions as I wrote, "I'm going to write 'the.' Watch me. 't, h, e'—that spells 'the.' It's a word you'll learn very quickly because you'll read and write it so often!

(handwritten sample on lined paper:)

Good EVENing!

This is our ✗ CLASSROOM •

WE WOD LiKE TO

SHOW YOU AROUND

the ROOM •

THANK YOU FOR

COMing

Love,

Mr. Halpern's

Class

(heart drawn)

The child who came up to write *CLASSROOM* began writing well below the line and so she made an *X* on it and began again.

Using the words *like, to, you,* and *for* gave me more opportunities to teach into future high-frequency words.

I had the child listen to the beginning and ending sounds in *room* and write them while I offered the vowels.

Using all capital letters is typical in September. In the interests of time and confidence-building, I didn't correct it.

We were out of time, so I quickly wrote the salutation at the end.

After watching the first child talk about and then write the *-ing* in *Evening*, I had a hunch a few children might remember this common ending. We approached *come* as a CVC word, and then the writer I called up added the *-ing* (which he did remember) at the end.

[W]riting instruction that encourages phonemic segmentation and invented spelling provides a rich context for developing the phonemic awareness and alphabetic knowledge children require for early reading.

(Craig 2003)

VIDEO 2.5: *Flexibility in Interactive Writing*

Flexible and Responsive Teaching Moves

Even when you establish a solid purpose for interactive writing, preplan some or all of your chart, and think carefully about which children to call up to write which parts, your students will almost always throw you curve balls. And who doesn't love a curve ball? Remember that the beauty of interactive writing is that the instruction for each child can be specific and targeted, and scaffolding can be added (or released) in process. The more interactive writing you do, the better you'll get at taking children's unexpected ideas, questions, and hesitancies, and flipping them into logical extensions and teaching points. The key is to remain flexible and ready to pivot in response to children's actions. Here are some possibilities:

IF...

A child is unsure of the sound(s) they hear in a word

THEN...

Ask them to say the word slowly, then again, and listen for the sound.

OR...

Ask them to listen to you (or another student) say the word slowly and listen for the sound.

IF...

A child is unsure how to write a letter

THEN...

Offer hand-over-hand or write it in a highlighter or light marker and have them trace it.

OR...

Model writing the letter off the paper and have them copy as you verbalize the letter pathway.

IF...

A child feels nervous or unsteady writing in front of the class

THEN...

Ask them to write a single letter and then offer them the option of sitting back down.

OR...

Try to coach them through feeling unsure and being brave.

IF...

A child makes a mistake (with spelling, spacing, etc.), notices it, and wants to correct it

THEN...

The simplest and most efficient way to correct is to cross out the mistake and write the correction above or next to it, depending on space. This strategy shows students how to make the correction quickly and without any special tools.

OR...

If the piece is for the public or there is no space to write the correction near it, I will use fix-it tape. I try to use this sparingly because I don't want to send the message that we need a special tool (even an eraser) to fix mistakes and keep writing.

IF...

A child asks a question about conventional vs. developmental spelling ("Is that the right way to spell it?")

THEN...

Think about purpose and audience. If the piece is for students and the spelling makes sense, explain, "When we're learning to write we write what we hear, and Rebecca hears /V/. What do you hear?"

OR...

If the spelling of the word is important (based on purpose and audience and/or the type of word—think high-frequency words), simply offer the correct spelling. "That's on our word wall! Who can help us spell 'went'?"

IF...

A child knows more of the word (sounds, spelling) than you anticipated

THEN...

Celebrate this knowledge and tie it back to teaching and practice.

OR...

Invite them to write more.

IF...

A child who is in a more advanced spelling stage verbally calls out and corrects a child writing

THEN...

If you know this might happen, have a conversation beforehand and remind them during the session, "It is so amazing you can spell many harder words already. If someone else is working to spell something and you know it's not right, let's not shout it out, so they can do their own best thinking. Why don't you give me a silent signal when you know, a thumbs up? A wink? What would you prefer?"

OR...

If this happens spontaneously and you were not able to have the conversation prior, you want to honor the thinking of the child who knows the conventional spelling without shaming the child working with you. You might say, "Yes, that is how you see this word spelling in books, isn't it? Right now, we're working on writing all the sounds we hear." Make sure to follow up with the child afterwards and set them up for a silent signal next time.

VIDEO 2.6: *Rereading and Rethinking*

Reread and Rethink

Experienced writers spend a lot of time rereading what they've written—and not just when they are finished. Right now, as I am writing this book, I will go back and read sentences and entire sections again and again. Each time I circle back, I find opportunities to:

☀ *Revise* to make my meaning clearer.

☀ *Edit* to make my text more conventional.

☀ *Think ahead* about what I'll write next based on what I've already written.

Beginning writers need this process of rereading modeled and scaffolded for them often during interactive writing so they'll begin to do it in their independent writing. I literally layer rereading across the entire interaction—we reread after each word, each phrase or sentence, and after the piece is complete. And each time we reread I model how the process can support children when they're writing on their own. Let's revisit our two examples and I'll show you what that modeling sounds like.

> **Rereading, getting a sense of how a text is working as a whole before you add more to it, is arguably the most important process skill a writer needs.**
> **(Ray and Cleaveland 2018)**

Once we determine the title, we read each word as we write it, then we go back and reread each word (cumulatively) before writing the next. "Let's read what we have. 'When can I . . .' What was next? Yes, 'interrupt' is the next word. When we go back and reread what we've written, it can help us remember what comes next!"

After the heavy lifting of listening and recording sounds in a single word, we always reread it, often more than once. "What does this word say?" "Let's point at the word as we read it." "Turn to your partner and read the word."

We reread high-frequency words to review them.

When we're finished, we reread the entire piece. It's a celebration and an opportunity to rethink (revise and edit) if we want.

Rereading gives us an opportunity to think about punctuation. "How should we say this when we read it? Do we need a period, question mark, or exclamation mark? What do you think? Turn and tell your partner."

We can listen for where sentences stop and start. "Let's read this sentence together. Does this sound like the end of the sentence? What do we need?"

After we determine what to write, we orally rehearse it before writing. "How many words do you hear? Say them and put a finger up for each word with me." Then, to help with the flow of ideas, we reread the phrase before adding a new word to it. "What word comes next? Let's go back and reread."

Rereading the entire piece gives children reading practice so they can share the writing with others. "Wow, we wrote a letter to our families! Let's practice reading it together while I point. Do you think you could read it to someone in your family later?" "Let's practice again." "Take turns reading the letter to your partner."

Every lesson is an apprenticeship in learning to write.

(Williams 2018)

Revise to Make the Meaning Clearer

Revision is the process, basically, of making the writing better—of making it do the work it's meant to do. Writers add, cut, replace, and move words, sentences, and whole sections around when they revise. In interactive writing, you'll find lots of opportunities to model the thinking of revision both as you're planning new text and rereading what you've already written. For example, you might revise:

OPPORTUNITIES TO MODEL REVISION

IDEAS

"What could the title of our chart be? Hmm . . . let's think about that. Turn and tell your partner an idea that you have."

"What would someone who is visiting our classroom need to know? Can you think of anything else we might add?"

REFINEMENTS

"Now that we've reread this, it seems like 'vomit' and 'being sick' are sort of the same thing. Maybe we should get rid of one of them."

WORD CHOICE

"Hmm . . . 'bother' makes sense. What other words could we use instead of 'bother'? 'Disturb'? 'Interrupt'? Which do you think is the best word for what we mean?"

"If we just say 'blood' it could mean a tiny bug bite. Is that enough? What else could we say that sounds more serious?"

ORGANIZATION

"We've got lots of ideas. What do you think we should say first?"

"I wonder if we should have put this at the end? We could cut it and move it there."

"I think we should write this word in big bold letters so it stands out."

Edit to Make the Text More Conventional

As children learn more about letters, sounds, and conventions, we expect them to use what they're learning in both interactive and independent writing. However, just as we don't expect babies to go from crawling to running a marathon, we don't expect beginning writers to suddenly start producing perfectly edited writing. Children can learn a lot, but even using all they know when they write, their texts will still be filled with approximations.

The key is to remember that as writers begin the process of putting thoughts on paper, we want them, more than anything, to write! And then write more! Roadblocks, obstacles, and self-doubt are the enemy of writing. So even though interactive writing is filled with opportunities to edit and fix mistakes, I know that children can't edit (on their own) for what they don't yet know. So, I keep my modeling of the editing process light, and I focus on helping children edit for what I think they do know (or almost know) because I've taught it. After all, if interactive writing is a time to model all the behaviors I want students to mirror during independent writing, I have to show them that mistakes are not only acceptable— they are part of the process.

VIDEO 2.7: *Editing to Make the Text More Conventional —A Light Touch*

Interactive writing enables students to: acquire foundational concepts about print, understand that writing is about communicating a message, apply rereading strategies to predict and monitor reading, articulate words slowly and hear and record letters in words, use simple resources as self-help tools, become fluent with correct letter formation, build a core of HF [high-frequency] words, cross-check multiple sources of information.

(Dorn and Soffos 2011)

TIP!

Remember! Editing should happen as children are ready for it, not from the start, and not all at once. If students are pressured to think about all these corrections before they are comfortable with writing, they'll never begin!

Learning awakens a variety of internal developmental processes that are able to operate only when the child is interacting with people in his environment and in cooperation with his peers.

(Vygotsky 1978)

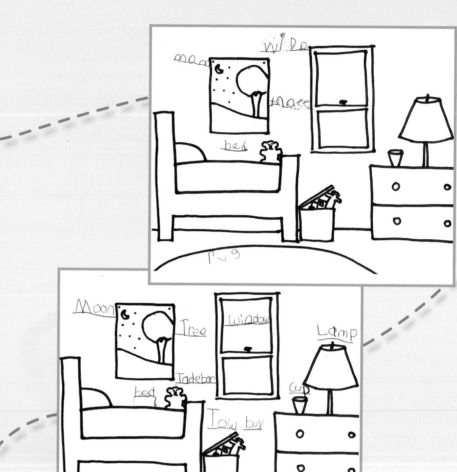

A Teacher's Guide to Interactive Writing

OPPORTUNITIES TO MODEL EDITING

HIGH-FREQUENCY WORDS

"Wait, 'look'! Do we need to sound that word out? How do you spell 'look'? Where could we look if we weren't sure. Ha! Yes, where can we look for 'look'?"

"Oh, 'in'! Let's see, you wrote 'en.' Does that look right? Let's check the word wall."

INDIVIDUAL SOUNDS

" 'Fire' . . . what do we hear at the beginning? Hmm, is it a 'V'? Watch my lips as I say the word slowly and listen carefully for the very first sound you hear . . . /f/. What do you think?"

DIGRAPHS, BLENDS, AND SPELLING PATTERNS

"Listen to me say 'blood' slowly. What two letters do you hear at the beginning?"

"The word is 'show' and there are two letters at the beginning that work together to make a different sound. It's not 'th' but you're on the right track—can someone help?"

"We sounded out the first part of the word 'come' but we want to write 'coming.' There are some friends who have been working on this with me in reading. Who can help us?"

HANDWRITING AND WORD PLACEMENT

"Let's fix that 'p' so it's pointing the right way, otherwise it looks like a nine. Do you want some help?"

"Let's get our letters on the line. Put a line through the 'C' and let's try again."

Word-Solving Opportunities

With interactive writing, you'll find endless opportunities to model, scaffold, and practice word solving—all the ways readers decode and all the ways writers encode. As you reread the texts you create with your students, voice over and reiterate important reading and writing strategies.

"Do you see a high-frequency word in this word? Turn and tell your partner what you see. Yes! 'In' is in the word 'interrupt.' That can help you write and read it!"

"Let's look at the letters. What is the first sound? The next? What could the word be?"

"Look at the second part of the word. There are three letters and three sounds, let's make them—/m/ /i/ /t/. Let's blend them . . . /mit/—yes!"

WeN Can I
intrupt Mr. Halpern?

 Fire

 LIts OV BLOOD

 THROW UP

 ker mit wucks in

"Listen to the word 'can.' Do you hear another high-frequency word we know when I say it? Listen to the end of the word—/c/ /an/. Yes, 'an'! And there are lots of words we can make with 'an'—'can, ban, fan, ran'..."

"Let's clap the syllables in 'Kermit'—Ker/mit. How many did you hear? Yes, two. The first part, /Ker/—how many sounds do you hear? Write them."

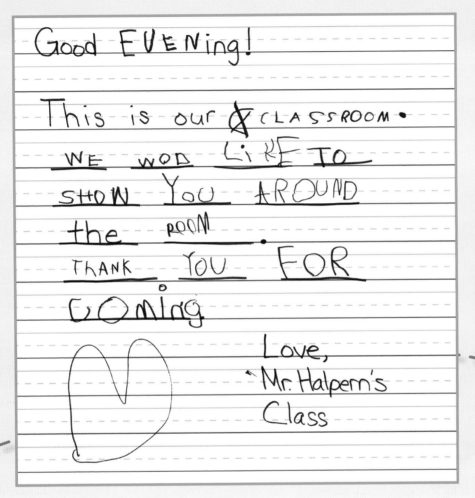

Good EVENing!

This is our ~~a~~ CLASSROOM.

WE WOD LiKE TO

SHOW YOU AROUND

the ROOM.

THANK YOU FOR

COMing

Love,
Mr. Halpern's
Class

"Hmm, 'we' is a high-frequency word we haven't learned yet, but it sounds a lot like another word we have learned. Yes—'me'! So, if we know how to write and read 'me,' we can also write and read 'we.'"

"Listen to me say this word slowly—/th/ /a/ /n/ /k/. What do you hear first? Watch my lips as I make the sound—/th/. What digraph makes that sound?"

"If you don't remember this word, let's try reading the sentence and think about what makes sense."

For students to apply the knowledge and skills they learn in one context to another, they must recognize the similarities between the two.

(Williams 2018)

Summarize

At the end of an interactive writing session, take a few moments (a minute or two, tops) to summarize the key takeaways. In these metacognitive moments, you show children what happens "under the hood" and help them prioritize, engage, and have agency in their learning.

IN THE SESSION, IF YOU . . .	THEN . . .
Introduced a new skill or statgey	Revisit the key details.
Reinforced an existing skill or strategy you want students to practice	Promote the transfer to independent reading and writing.
Reviewed skills and strategies you feel most kids know	Highlight the importance of student engagement in interactive writing.

SOMETIMES, A QUICK RECAP WILL INCLUDE MORE THAN ONE KIND OF SUMMARY. CONSIDER EXAMPLES LIKE THESE:

"Writers, wasn't this fun? When we stop and write together, we help each other learn. Authors do that! They help each other be better. You can do this when you're writing by yourself too. What's one way we helped a friend during interactive writing today that you could use to help a friend at your table during writing workshop?"

"Let's review our chart. It says to be flexible you have to have more than one plan. It shows Plan A, Plan B—read them with me—Plan C, and Plan D. Hmm . . . so during Choice Time today, if you wanted to go to Blocks and it was full, you'd have to be . . . Yes, flexible! How could you be flexible? Turn and tell your partner."

This summary is specific in detailing the importance of the work, but also asks children to take ownership of skills and strategies scaffolded. The language encourages them to try out and/or practice key learning during independent reading and writing.

"Writers, did you notice all the high-frequency words we wrote and used today? We wrote a few on our chart. Can you find one and whisper it to your partner? And then there were other words that had high-frequency words inside them. Can you find one of those and whisper it to your partner? Do you see how knowing these words can help you when you go to write? You can use the words you know and the word wall to help you!"

Instead of writing skills, this quick summary is all about reviewing the content of the chart. The clock was ticking, and I wanted to make sure we reviewed the key learning—being flexible—before moving into Choice Time, where I'm looking for kids to practice this social skill.

While we covered multiple skills and strategies in the session, this summary briefly highlights just one of them and reminds children to take it back to their independent work. A clear focus in the summary helps children internalize the learning and gives it a better chance to stick. Just be sure to vary which strategies you highlight each time you recap.

VIDEO 2.8: *Extending the Learning*

Extend the Learning

Part of the magic with interactive writing is that after you are finished with the process, you have a beautiful product to use in your teaching. Unlike a chart you bought or created yourself, your interactive writing charts and posters will hold extra meaning for students because they had a literal hand in constructing them. Here are a few examples of ways to utilize all the pieces you'll create during interactive writing:

* **Shared Reading.** Reading pieces together as a class is the perfect way to revisit content, practice reading strategies, and transfer both to independent reading and writing.

* **Independent Reading.** Students benefit from having short texts they can read independently, especially early in the year, and pieces you've created and then read together many times are perfect. One simple way to get these into kids' hands is to photograph them (keep it simple, use your phone) and then print and copy for each student.

* **Anchor Charts.** Ah, those routines, procedures, strategies, skills, and all the important information that you want to review—often.

* **Illustrations.** Just like anything else we read, illustrations can help us remember the text we write together during interactive writing. The problem is, of course, creating illustrations takes precious time. Here are a few ways to illustrate pieces:

  * **Before:** I will illustrate or print out pictures, cut them out, and we'll add them as we create the text.

  * **Before:** Illustrations are on the chart but covered up and then revealed when we are ready.

  * **During:** Depending on what the picture is, either I or a student can do a quick sketch if it's simple. Basic shapes, simple faces, etc., all lend themselves to real-time illustrating.

- **After:** Regardless of who sketches the illustration during the session, I often will ask a student to finish it and/or color it afterward.
- **After:** Sometimes, I will simply ask a child to add illustrations after the session is over (at another time of the day—arrival, snack, choice time, etc.).

* **Displays.** Here's a little gift interactive writing can give you: you'll never have to spend time creating bulletin boards again! You can either plan a session to create a display ("I was thinking we could create a bulletin board display together . . . ") or you can use something you created for some other reason (science and social studies charts often lend themselves to this).

* **Mentor Texts.** With interactive writing, almost every piece becomes a mentor text— something students can return to over and over again to help them remember skills and strategies they use in their independent reading and writing. All of the risk-taking, scaffolding, and teaching from the interactive writing session lives on in the piece afterwards.

SET THE PURPOSE

THINK ABOUT THE AUDIENCE

COMPOSE AND CONSTRUCT THE TEXT

REREAD AND RETHINK

SUMMARIZE

EXTEND THE LEARNING

VIDEO 3.1: *Informing Interactive Writing Sessions with Formal Assessments*

[M]ost of [these lessons] came about based on having observed, talked with, and listened to our students during conferences and from having studied their work and observed their ways of working.

(Horn and Giacobbe 2007)

Research! Information from Independent Writing That Informs Interactive Writing

WHILE IT IS CRITICAL TO BE FLEXIBLE AND RESPONSIVE WHEN using interactive writing (our students always surprise us!) researching your students' needs is truly a valuable way to give your sessions added depth and increased efficacy. There are many ways to find teaching points to focus on during interactive writing. Let's dig into some of them.

Formal Assessments

I have found that the most helpful formal assessments to inform our interactive writing sessions are Concepts About Print, Letter/Sound ID, and High-Frequency Words. These assessments are widely available with most literacy curricula or through a simple internet search. These kinds of assessments will help you, especially at the beginning of the year, when your students are most likely not doing a whole lot of conventional writing. Being able to pinpoint what strategies and skills you need to hit quickly and hardest during interactive writing right out of the gate will make your sessions lean and purposeful.

ASSESSMENT	STRATEGIES/SKILLS TO TEACH DURING INTERACTIVE WRITING

Concepts About Print

Print carries the message: If children don't know this coming to school, they will learn it quickly as you read and write together. You'll explicitly tell them "the words are what we read," and every time you finish a piece you'll ask them to "read what we wrote together."

Direction of print and return sweep: As we read and write, we will explicitly show children where we start on the paper, which way we read/write (left to right), and what to do when we get to the end of writing/reading a line (move down one line and start at the left side).

Difference between letter/word: In our first sessions, we will talk about what letters are and how words are made up of letters/sounds. We'll use interactive writing to informally assess whether or not students can identify letters and words, often before we formally assess them.

One-to-One Correspondence: As we read our writing, we will be pointing under each word. Every. Single. Time. Long before we teach this skill explicitly during reading workshop, our students will have practice with it.

Punctuation: As we write, we will talk about punctuation. We will teach about what comes at the end of sentences and expose our students to all forms of punctuation.

Letter/Sound ID

Looking at what letters/sounds our class knows and needs to learn will directly impact our sessions. We will start with the letters in children's names. We will create lots of opportunities to study and write these letters during interactive writing. As children learn more letters/sounds, we will continue to watch for students with deficits and make sure those children are called on often to practice saying/writing/reading those letters/sounds during interactive writing.

High-Frequency Words

As we teach and assess high-frequency words, we'll take note of specific student strengths and challenges, and create lots of opportunities during interactive writing for those words to be practiced.

Informal Observations

Teachers are watchers. One of our biggest jobs is to observe our students and use the information we gather to guide our teaching. While formal assessments are important, they typically don't happen often and are only a snapshot of what a child is able to produce on a given day at a given time.

So, it is our informal observations that truly bring to light what our students are able to put into practice: what is transferring, and, most importantly, sticking for students, and what is not?

INFORMAL OBSERVATIONS OF WRITING

INTERACTIVE WRITING

Interactive writing provides the highest level of scaffolding. By its very nature, we, the teachers, are positioned to help support and lift the level of the writing. There are times when I will step back and let a child work on their own as the class and I watch. There are also prompts where I will ask whether support is needed. This in itself is a wonderful way to informally assess.

* "Do you need help?"
* "You have an 's' in your name. I bet you know how to write it. Give it a try."
* "Hmm, we are writing the high-frequency word 'look.' Do you know how to spell that? If not, where could you look?"

INDEPENDENT WRITING

In addition to actual writing conferences (see below), sometimes we walk around and watch as children write—sometimes not saying a word, but simply observing what they do when left to their own devices. As the children begin writing, I often like to wait five minutes or so before I begin conferring. I want to see what they do when truly writing independently. How do they start? Are they always starting a new piece? What tools do they use? Do they always start with a picture? Are they hesitant to begin? All this information informs our interactive writing sessions.

ANY OTHER WRITING HAPPENING DURING THE DAY

Lots of writing happens in a classroom outside of writing workshop, during reading, math, science, social studies, etc. It is helpful to pay attention to what skills and strategies children carry over. It is not uncommon for beginning writers to put newly learned strategies into play during writing workshop, but then forget them outside of the workshop time. This is one reason to utilize interactive writing throughout the day. Writing together during all academic areas not only offers more practice with essential skills and strategies, but also reminds children that authors do these things whenever they write.

Children can imitate a variety of actions that go well beyond the limits of their own capabilities. Using imitation, children are capable of doing much more in collective activity or under the guidance of adults.

(Vygotsky 1978)

Conferences

When you cozy up next to a writer to look at their work, often a big part of the writing conference is doing a little research. What does this writer need to help push them to the next level in their writing? How can I utilize interactive writing to create effective scaffolds that help students reach the next level in their independent writing? What we often find is that our youngest writers need so many teaching points it can feel overwhelming. By utilizing interactive writing within conferences, we can focus on a single strategy, but also weave in others as they arise.

Using What You Know to Help You Plan

Let's look at the trajectory of two children's writing over time, and how what we notice about our students' writing can be supported by interactive writing work. As you will see, there is no set timeline for teaching strategies. Children will grasp ownership of them when they are ready—and that will be different for each student! Knowing what our students need will help us layer strategies into our interactive writing and continue to cycle back to repeat them as needed.

VIDEO 3.2: *Ruby's and Harrison's Growth*

What to Notice

Ruby is drawing her family and labeling each member. She knows how to spell their names and feels comfortable writing them. This is relatively low risk for her.

What to Notice

Ruby is starting to write a sentence. She knows where the words for the sentence go and she's writing some of the sounds she hears.

Implications for Interactive Writing

✴ Focus on taking risks
✴ Repeated practice with saying words and writing the sounds we hear
✴ Simple sentence construction using high-frequency words and shorter words.

Implications for Interactive Writing

✴ Continued work on stretching words to hear and record more sounds
✴ Strategies for hearing and recording words (counting words on fingers, drawing lines for words, etc.).

What to Notice

Ruby knows using high-frequency words can help her construct her thoughts more clearly. She also is leaving a space after each word! She continues to understand how labeling can help her piece.

What to Notice

Ruby has learned many new high-frequency words and is using them in her writing! She is hearing/recording many sounds when she writes, including the /th/ digraph. She also is learning to edit her work for mistakes.

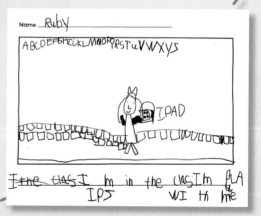

Implications for Interactive Writing

✴ Continued teaching and practicing existing and new high-frequency words in pieces we compose together
✴ Strategies for writing longer sentences (repeating the sentence often, rereading after each word is written).

Implications for Interactive Writing

✴ Continued work on editing our work together
✴ Continued teaching/practice of digraphs during interactive writing
✴ Continued teaching/practice of ending punctuation.

What to Notice

Harrison is beginning to explore labeling.

Implications for Interactive Writing

✳ Strategies for labeling: where the label goes, how to plan for the label (drawing lines, spacing, etc.)

✳ Continued practice with saying/stretching words to hear/record sounds.

What to Notice

Harrison now has strategies for labeling. He is beginning to explore writing a sentence at the bottom of his piece.

Implications for Interactive Writing

✳ Strategies for hearing/recording words (counting words on fingers, repeating sentence after writing each word, drawing lines for each word, tapping each line as we say the word).

What to Notice

Harrison is having fun with his labels. He has created his own strategy for spaces between words! The vertical line after each word shows he's thinking about the need to put something between his words.

Implications for Interactive Writing

✳ Continued teaching/practice of strategies for leaving a space. In addition to teaching these in a whole group, I work with Harrison in a small group to fine-tune his method.

What to Notice

Harrison is learning high-frequency words and adding them to his labels and sentences. He is experimenting with new strategies to leave a space (using his finger and drawing a line).

Implications for Interactive Writing

✳ Continued teaching/practice of existing/new high-frequency words
✳ Continued teaching/practice with leaving a space
✳ Teaching/practice of ending punctuation.

Planning to Support Group Needs

As you sit with students and study their habits along with formal assessments, overarching themes often appear. These will shift as your students grow, of course, but you will usually be able to identify similar needs among groups of students. When those teaching points become clear, interactive writing is a perfect tool to teach a small group or even the entire class these overarching necessities.

USING WHAT YOU KNOW ABOUT <u>GROUP</u> NEEDS TO PLAN FOR INTERACTIVE WRITING

IF YOU SEE THIS OVERARCHING NEED → **CREATE THESE OPPORTUNITIES DURING INTERACTIVE WRITING**

No letters or sounds, random letter strings, text copied from around the room, etc.

Create lots of initial sound work: opportunities for children to say a word, listen for the first sound, identify the letter on the alphabet chart, and write it. Try to focus on shorter, simple words. Much of the interactive writing at the beginning of the school year is initial sound work.

No spaces between words

At some point in kindergarten, this will be a need for all your students! I like to teach different strategies and let children pick what works best for them. Counting words and drawing lines for each; using your finger to leave a space after each word; and sliding the pencil/pen after each word are a few go-to strategies for leaving a space.

Initial sounds only

This can become the meat of interactive writing. We are brave spellers! We say words slowly, stretch them out, listen for as many sounds as we can hear, and write them all. For students who are challenged by this, we start by focusing on simple, short words with only a few sounds.

No (or few) vowels

Focusing on vowels is a continual process. As we work together on pieces, I will constantly be teaching, reteaching, and reviewing vowel sounds. Repetition is key, especially with vowel sounds that often get confused (short i and e).

Planning to Support Individual Needs

Conversely, as we confer with students, individual needs will arise. Those may look similar to the overarching themes but may apply only to an individual student. Interactive writing can be used as a tool during a conference or small group to teach into a strategy. You may also take that information into your whole-group interactive writing sessions and use it to help select specific students for tasks.

As you can see, most needs you observe can be layered into interactive writing. The more you watch your students write and reflect on what you see, the more ideas you will have for interactive writing!

USING WHAT YOU KNOW ABOUT <u>INDIVIDUAL</u> NEEDS TO PLAN FOR INTERACTIVE WRITING

IF YOU SEE THIS INDIVIDUAL STUDENT IS WRITING ·····························▶ **CREATE THIS OPPORTUNITY FOR THE STUDENT DURING INTERACTIVE WRITING**

No letters or sounds, random letter strings, text copied from around the room, etc.

Regardless of where the rest of the class is, it can be helpful for students to come up and simply say the word, identify the initial sound, identify the corresponding letter on the alphabet chart, and write it. Having this complex process broken down, modeled, and done in a collaborative manner with the teacher can be supportive to children needing work on this strategy.

No spaces between words

Some children need more practice. This is a good opportunity to let them come up and work with you to count words and draw lines before starting a sentence. I also will select these children to do the spacing work after they finish a word.

Initial sounds only

What many children need most is repeated, scaffolded, supported practice saying words, and then identifying and writing as many sounds as they can. If children are writing initial sounds only, I will often ask them to do this work in a targeted way with shorter words. Small two-letter words that are often high-frequency words (it, is, me, up, us, we, etc.) work well, as do CVC words with clearly differentiated sounds (cat, sit, hop, pen, cup, etc.).

No (or few) vowels

Once we have sufficiently studied vowels and children know that every word has at least one vowel, we create opportunities to listen for vowels in words. We study each vowel and its sounds, and then we decide which vowel we hear and write it. At first, children often hear the wrong vowel but, depending on the purpose of and audience for our piece, we write what we hear and move on.

Evidence It's Working! What to Look for in Independent Writing to Know Your Teaching Is Sticking

Of course, the goal of all of this is for our teaching to stick—to become incorporated into children's writing processes, and to be part of the repertoire of writing strategies and skills that they use in any writing context. While that is the goal, it doesn't always happen at the pace we'd like, so here are some tips to help the teaching stick.

Transfer of Skills and Strategies

As you continue to work with students during interactive writing, small groups, and individual conferences, how will you know your teaching is working? Well, quite simply, you're going to look to see the skills and strategies you've taught transferring to independent writing. You'll look for those spaces between words. You'll notice what strategies children are using to remember those spaces. You'll ask questions to find out how they're remembering or inquire why they've done it a certain way. The observation process is truly a cycle. You'll meet students where they are, teaching and reinforcing them, and then you will continue to lift the level of each student's work. You'll continue to think about what you see and how it can inform your teaching—specifically, what you need to include in your interactive writing.

OBSERVATION CYCLE

OBSERVING
during whole group, small group, individual conferences: noticing, noting, inquiring, describing

ANALYZING:
Thinking, wondering about observations. What do they tell us about what children know? What do they need to know next?

PLANNING:
What's next for this child? Small group? Whole class? What strategies and skills will most benefit them? What experiences offer opportunities to teach and practice those strategies?

When teachers shift participation structures in the context of group writing events, they prepare students for taking up author roles when writing independently.

(Williams 2018)

What If It's Not Sticking?

What if it's not sticking? What if, after all my planning, teaching, and reteaching, certain strategies aren't transferring into children's independent writing work? Let us not underestimate the power of reteaching! Most scientists agree that children need to be exposed to new learning many, many times before committing it to habit (Zhan, et al. 2018). Some children will only need to be taught something new one or two times while others will need to be exposed many more times. The answer is that every child is different and sometimes simply reteaching a strategy one more time will do the trick. The number of times teachers need to teach into proper capitalization is proof of this!

The good news is it won't hurt anyone to hear a strategy taught again. We can't be afraid to reteach, sometimes many times, to students. While we will reteach strategies during interactive writing many times, one way to lift the level is to involve those students who show they grasp the strategy in the reteaching. Calling on students to be teachers not only helps them internalize their own learning, but it also helps other students hear the strategy in (sometimes) a new way and (always) a new voice.

RETEACHING: STUDENTS AS TEACHERS

WHOLE GROUP

Teacher: Writers, we've been working so hard to make our writing easier for others to read and today, Nora is going to come up and show us one way she's doing that by leaving spaces between her words. Nora, how are you remembering to leave spaces between words?

Nora: When I get to the end of a word, before I say the next one, I slide my hand over. Before I listen for the first sound of the next word, I listen for the slide.

Nora demonstrates her technique on the piece we're creating together. We all listen for the slide.

SMALL GROUP

I have gathered a small group of four students on the carpet. They all are struggling with leaving spaces between words, except for Ivy. Ivy is my helper in this small group. Much as during the whole group interactive writing session, I will guide the small group in creating a piece together. This may happen over the course of a few days.

Day 1: We sketch and label our pictures.

Day 2: We write a short, simple sentence on each page (this is where I might invite my helper).

Day 3: We add another short, simple sentence to each page together.

PARTNERSHIPS

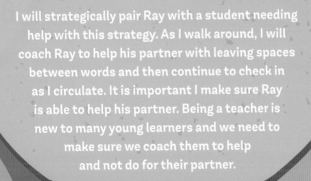

I will strategically pair Ray with a student needing help with this strategy. As I walk around, I will coach Ray to help his partner with leaving spaces between words and then continue to check in as I circulate. It is important I make sure Ray is able to help his partner. Being a teacher is new to many young learners and we need to make sure we coach them to help and not do for their partner.

VIDEO 3.4: *Coaching into Partnerships*

Working together, this partnership wrote "CLOC" by saying the word slowly, multiple times, as one wrote the letters with a pencil. Then, once written, the other traced the word with a marker as they both said each sound again.

Teaching, observing, and reteaching will continue as we build our students' toolboxes of strategies. While the need to be flexible in our teaching continues, the more we research our students, the more purposeful our interactive writing sessions will be.

Another way for students to help their peers using interactive writing is by simply instructing one to be the writer and the other to be a tracer. When I have a child who really struggles with the fine motor aspects of writing, tracing is a great way to build hand strength while practicing the handwriting pathways.

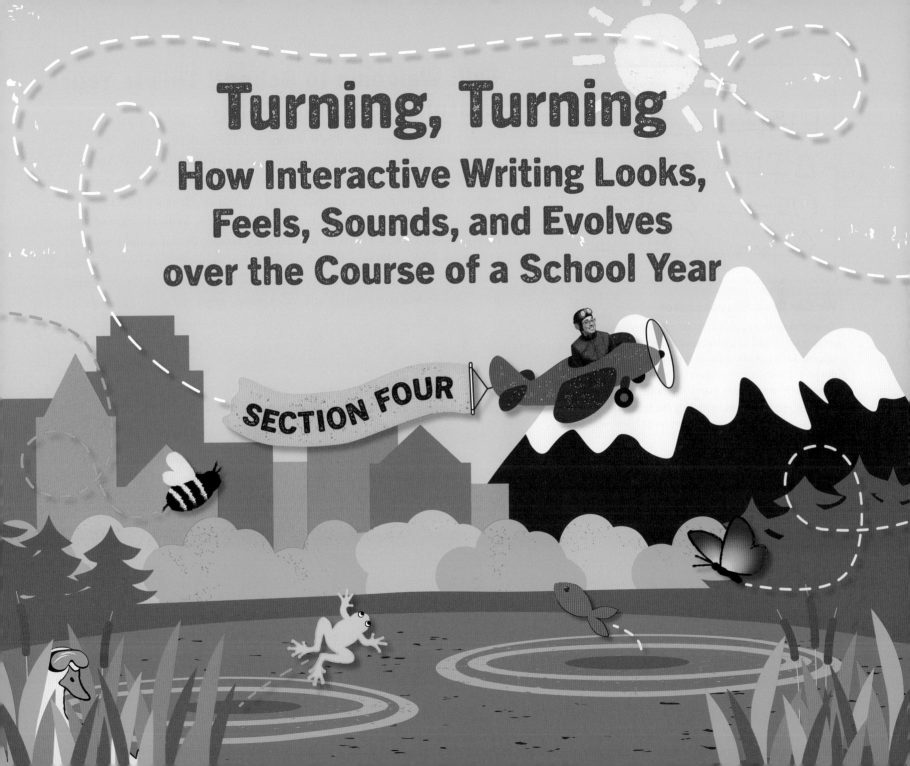

Turning, Turning
How Interactive Writing Looks, Feels, Sounds, and Evolves over the Course of a School Year

SECTION FOUR

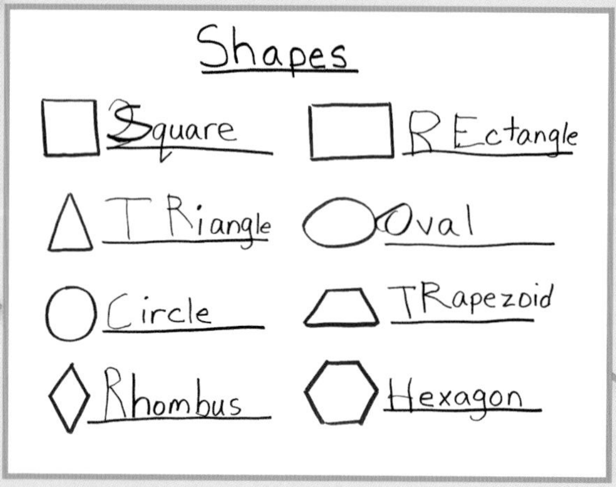

Shapes

☐ Square   ☐ REctangle

△ TRiangle   ⬭ Oval

◯ Circle   ⏢ TRapezoid

◇ Rhombus   ⬡ Hexagon

We Can Draw Shapes poster

This (or something similar) is one of the first interactive writing sessions I do as we identify, review, and name shapes. Ahead of the session, I've written the title and drawn the shapes. I then cover the shapes with paper and reveal each one as we're ready. This is so basic but adds mystery! Most children write only the first letter of each shape name, with a few exceptions for children who are ready to write more.

Fall: Welcome to School! This Is Your Learning and Your Space

There is nothing quite like a new school year for fresh beginnings. As we gather as a community for the first time, interactive writing allows us to learn about each other, class routines, and taking risks. These first precious months of school help me understand each child as a learner and, more importantly, as a human being. Beyond the academic skills they know and those I need to teach, I start to see how they tackle obstacles and how much I can push each of them within their individual zones of proximal development. Some children are ready for challenges from day one and others need more time to feel comfortable and safe taking bigger risks.

Pumpkin poster

Toward the end of fall, as our letter/sound knowledge increases, as a scaffold to having children label their own independent writing, we begin to label—everything. Here we labeled a giant pumpkin together before children did their own.

Empathy poster

In the fall, the first interactive writing we do usually has more of my writing on it than it will even just a few months later. Here, I've had children help me with the sounds in *empathy* (I gave the letters for /th/ because I knew this poster would be up all year and I wanted it spelled correctly. Alternatively, I could have not, and most likely the children would have suggested f. In that case, we would correct it later when learning digraphs. Either choice works.) It would sound something like this: "Hmm, what makes the /th/ sound?" Most children will not know in the fall so I'll interject with "It's actually two letters together that make the /th/ sound—'t' and 'h' make that sound, first 't' and then 'h.'"

Winter: Building on Fall's Foundations

With our routines set and relationships on their way, we begin to build on the foundational work of the fall. By now our concepts about print are mostly solid and we're able to utilize that knowledge as we write. New letters, sounds, and sight words are being added to our repertoire daily and we build those into our interactive writing. As children become braver, we push ourselves to do more. We work in partnerships to help each other and work on becoming teachers who help but do not tell.

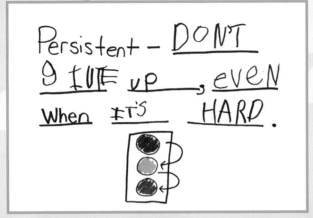

Persistent poster

As we continue our mindset work from the fall, I am now writing the name of the stance (Persistent) and having students write the rest of the definition. I wrote the word "When" because we were running short on time.

Mindset Self-Talk poster

Many children are now writing entire words, phrases, and even sentences when they come up. The tr in try is a tricky sound because it does often sound like /ch/ when we speak. I was happy because this revealed what they had learned already about digraphs when the ch was offered!

A Teacher's Guide to Interactive Writing

Library Bin labels

Working in small groups, children discussed what the name for each library bin should be and then wrote and illustrated their labels as I circulated and coached into each group.

Spring: Extending the Learning

By the spring, not only are the flowers blooming, but we are becoming fearless writers. Children come up and often say, "I don't need help"—and whether they actually need assistance or not, they are not the same hesitant, sometimes scared, students from the fall. We are writers! Longer words with more sounds are no obstacle for us! We are learning new skills in phonics, like blends and digraphs, and we are trying them out in our interactive writing together.

With summer looming, we are synthesizing all the strategies and skills from the school year to end with some magical interactive writing.

Parts of a Plant bulletin board

One of my favorite teacher hacks is having children create bulletin boards. We do all the work and learning as a class, and they help me decide how to put it all together. For this simple display, children helped me decide what words to use (dirt, soil, ground, etc.). After each label was written, students placed them on the board.

High-Frequency Words chart

As we learn more and more high-frequency words, we add them to our word wall, but often I like to have another place closer to our gathering area where we can read, add to, and play games with the words. We worked together to add the words already up on our word wall and then continued to add any new ones as we learned them.

Character poster

This poster, inspired by strategies in Jennifer Serravallo's *The Reading Strategies Book* (2015), shows the deep thinking work we're doing in the spring! In order to push students to think about characters in their reading, we created this together over three days. I drew the simple pictures on the sticky notes so we could add one each day and then the writing that went with it.

Characters

Name Wut the Character...

Does   Thinks/ Says feels

this character is the kinde of

person/animal who...

STUDY GUIDE A Teacher's Guide to Interactive Writing

To download this Study Guide, please visit http://hein.pub/Interactive and click on Companion Resources.

Digging into Section One: Welcome to Interactive Writing

* How do you feel about interactive writing?
* What questions do you have about interactive writing?

Creating a Space Where Interactive Writing Will Thrive

* If you're a new teacher, what message would you like to hear about teaching?
* If you're not a new teacher, what message would you give your new teacher self?
* How have you typically set up your classroom? What shifts would you like to consider?
* What vision do you have for your classroom space? What steps will help you achieve this?
* How do you envision interactive writing fostering community in your classroom?

Take a look at the early interactive writing session with kindergarteners that appears on pages 2–3.

* Which moves/prompts would you like to try with your students?
* How is Matt flexible with student responses?

Watch video 1.2, Interactive Writing vs. Shared Writing (see page 4).
Think about your own classroom and students. What work are you doing together now that might be best served by shared writing? What might be best served by interactive writing?

After you've read about each principle, think about how they fit in to your own classroom.

> **The Principles of Interactive Writing**
> Interactive writing:
> * is a *community* experience
> * gives writers a safe place to explore *risk-taking*
> * provides children *scaffolding* in the writing process
> * is *differentiated*
> * is *flexible* and *responsive*
> * *happens often.*

Watch video 1.6, Interactive Writing in Small Groups (see page 18).

* What do you notice about the way Matt interacts with students during the small group?
* What moves does he make to support each student's learning?

Watch video 1.7, Differentiation in Interactive Writing (see page 22).

* What are some ways Matt differentiates for each student?
* How is the experience the same for each student? How is it different?

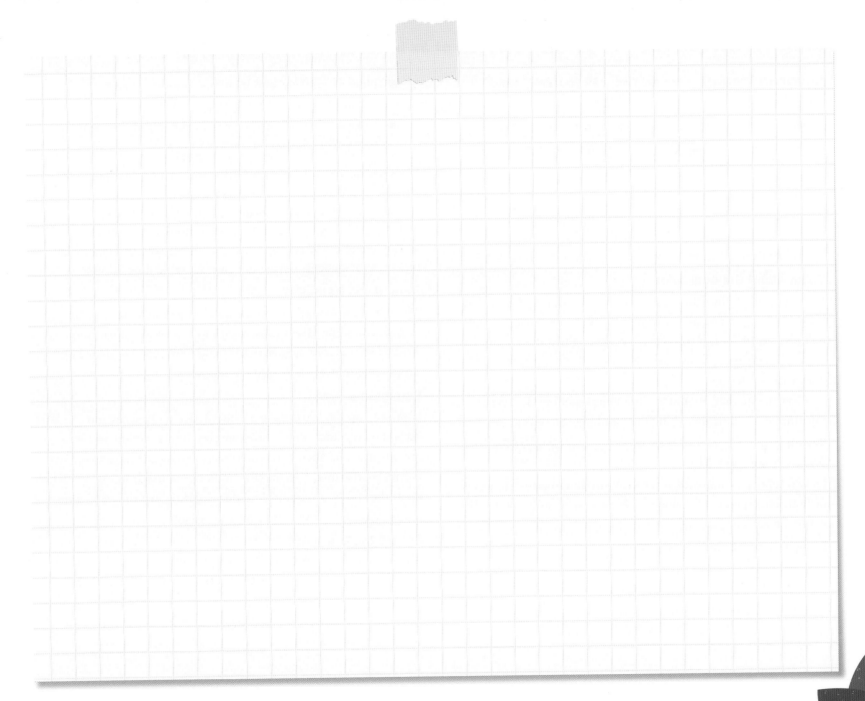

Exploring Section Two: The Predictable Flow of an Interactive Writing Session

As you read through Section Two, ask yourself these questions—or discuss with colleagues:

* How does interactive writing mirror the writing process?
* In what ways can we work to make this connection visible to children?

Set the Purpose

After reading this section, were any of the ideas for setting the purpose of interactive writing surprising to you? Are there any you'd like to try? Did you think of any others not described?

Think About the Audience

How do you see the difference between a writing audience that includes children and adults in your class, vs. an audience that includes people not in your class? What might shift in your interactive writing pieces as you consider different audiences with your students?

How do you feel about developmental spelling? Did any information in the book shift your thinking? How so?

Watch video 2.2, Science of Reading and Interactive Writing (see page 51).

How does the structure of Interactive Writing support all kinds of literacy instruction, including phonics work substantiated by reading research?

Compose and Construct the Text

After reading through this section, think about how all the elements of interactive writing come together as you and your students compose and construct text.

* How do you envision including both planned and unplanned interactive writing in your day?
* What are some ways you can be flexible and responsive to students during interactive writing?

Watch video 2.4, Layering Skills and Strategies into Interactive Writing Lessons (see page 56).

Interactive writing allows us to teach and reinforce many skills and strategies during a short amount of time by tucking them in as they come up. What are some of the skills and strategies Matt tackles with students during this interactive writing session?

Reread and Rethink

The opportunity to revise and edit our work can invite us to introduce and/or revisit important phonics work. What phonics work is your class doing currently, and how can you imagine supporting that work during interactive writing?

Summarize

Summing up the learning in an interactive writing session should be succinct. Read the examples in this section and note the purpose and brevity of each. Sometimes short and sweet is harder than it might seem. Do you notice yourself going on and on at the end of a session? Practice isolating just the important points and saying them as clearly as possible.

Extend the Learning

Think about your most recent interactive writing session. How could you build on that work? What new ideas would you like to try?

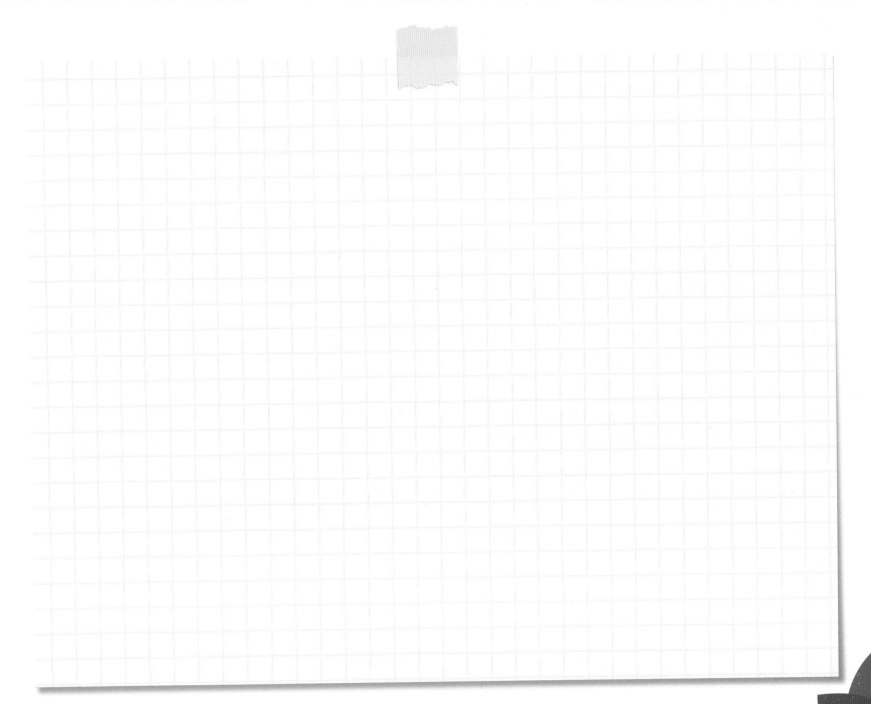

Investigating Section Three: Transfer to and from Writing Workshop

Interactive writing allows us to research what our students know and, more importantly, what we need to teach them. What can we learn from watching students write independently? How can we use that information to inform our interactive writing sessions?

Conferences

After reading over what to notice and the implications for teaching in Ruby's writing, look at Harrison's pieces and try to see what you notice and what teaching moves you might offer him before reading my thoughts. Additionally, choose several pieces from one of your own students to study—how might what you notice in your student's independent writing be supported in an interactive writing session?

Using What You Know About Group Needs to Plan for Interactive Writing

After reading this section, can you think of any other potential needs for the whole class or small group? How might you create opportunities for teaching them during interactive writing? Better yet, think about your own class—how could you use interactive writing to practice skills the whole class or a group of children need support with?

Observation Cycle

How might using the Observation Cycle (see page 87, or the figure at right) help support all students?

Thinking about either a single student, group of students, or your whole class, refer to the Observation Cycle.

INTERACTIVE WRITING ESSENTIALS

Observing	Analyzing	Planning
Describe what you notice?	What does what you're observing tell you about what the child/children know?	What strategies and skills will most benefit them?
Do you have any questions?	What do they need to know next?	What experiences offer opportunities to teach and practice those strategies?

Watch video 3.4, Coaching into Partnerships (see page 90).

- ✳ How does Matt coach students to help each other? What moves does he make?
- ✳ How does this process support both students' learning?

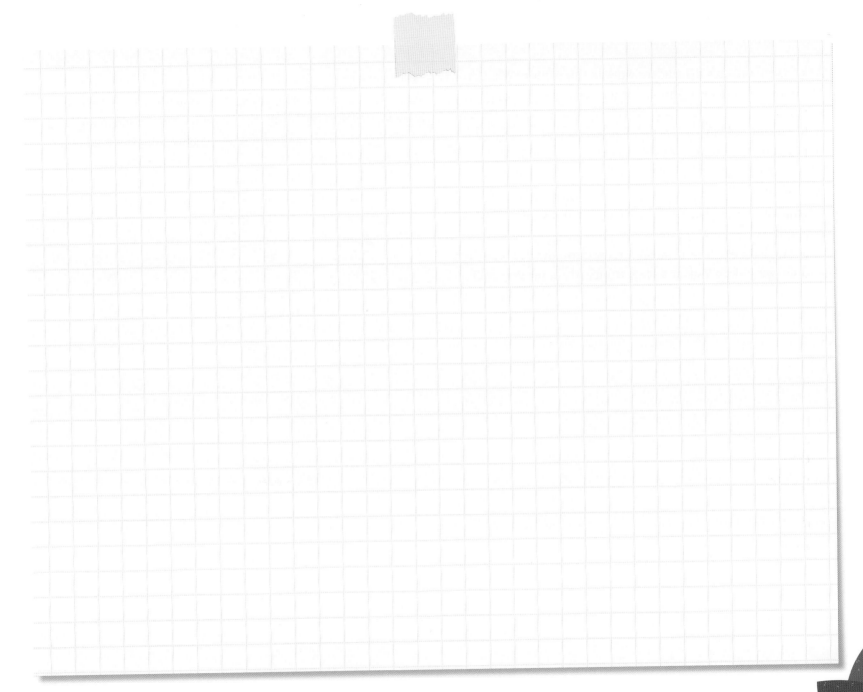

Examining Section Four: Turning, Turning

Take a spin through the student work in this section. What do you notice about how the pieces change and evolve through the year?

If you are new to interactive writing and have just started trying this work with your students, take a look at the first piece you've created together. What do you notice? What do your students already know? And what might come next in interactive writing? Do you have particular skills and strategies in mind that you might focus on?

If you have been doing interactive writing with your class for a while now, take a look at a piece from early in the year, and your most recent piece. Put them alongside each other, if you can. What do you notice about your students' growth? What might you focus on in your next interactive writing session?

If you are reading this book with colleagues, you might each bring a couple of interactive writing pieces to share. Discuss the growth you see, and think about what you might focus on next.

Now that you've gotten your feet wet with interactive writing, how has your thinking changed? How do you imagine including interactive writing in your classroom life?

At first I thought . . .

Now I think . . .

Peace Out!

WORKS CITED

Craig, Sharon. 2003. "The Effects of an Adapted Interactive Writing Intervention on Kindergarten Children's Phonological Awareness, Spelling, and Early Reading Development." *Reading Research Quarterly* 38 (4): 438–440.

Dorn, Linda J., and Carla Soffos. 2011. *Interventions that Work: A Comprehensive Intervention Model for Preventing Reading Failure in Grades K–3*. New York: Pearson.

Glover, Matt. 2020. "Supporting Spelling at Home." *Parent-to-Parent*, April 6. YouTube video, 10:24. https://www.youtube.com/watch?v=1KrjBBHRVBA.

Horn, Martha, and Mary Ellen Giacobbe. 2007. *Talking, Drawing, Writing: Lessons for Our Youngest Writers*. Portland, ME: Stenhouse.

Lindfors, Judith Wells. 2008. *Children's Language: Connecting Reading, Writing, and Talk*. New York: Teachers College Press.

McCarrier, Andrea, Gay Su Pinnell, and Irene C. Fountas. 2000. *Interactive Writing: How Language and Literacy Come Together, K–2*. Portsmouth, NH: Heinemann.

Mraz, Kristine, and Christine Hertz. 2015. *A Mindset for Learning: Teaching the Traits of Joyful, Independent Growth*. Portsmouth, NH: Heinemann.

Patterson, Elizabeth, Megan Schaller, and Jeannine Clemens. 2008. "A Closer Look at Interactive Writing." *Reading Teacher* 61 (6): 496–497.

Ray, Katie Wood, and Lisa B. Cleaveland. 2018. *A Teacher's Guide to Getting Started with Beginning Writers*. Portsmouth, NH: Heinemann.

Roberts, Theresa A. 2017. *Literacy Success for Emergent Bilinguals: Getting It Right in the PreK–2 Classroom*. New York: Teachers College Press.

Roth, Kate, and Joan Dabrowski. 2016. *Interactive Writing Across Grades: A Small Practice with Big Results*. Portland, ME: Stenhouse.

Serravallo, Jennifer. 2015. *The Reading Strategies Book: Your Everything Guide to Developing Skilled Readers*. Portsmouth, NH: Heinemann.

Vygotsky, L. S. 1978. *Mind in Society: The Development of Higher Psychological Processes*. Cambridge, MA: Harvard University Press.

Williams, Cheri. 2018. "Learning to Write with Interactive Writing Instruction." *The Reading Teacher* 71 (5): 523–532. https://doi.org/10.1002/trtr.1643.

Wood, D., J. S. Bruner, and Gail Ross. 1976. "The Role of Tutoring in Problem Solving." *Journal of Child Psychology and Psychiatry* 17: 89–100. Great Britain: Pergamon Press.

Zhan, L., D. Guo, G. Chen, and J. Yang. 2018. "Effects of Repetition Learning on Associative Recognition Over Time: Role of the Hippocampus and Prefrontal Cortex." *Frontiers in Human Neuroscience* 12 (July 11). doi: 10.3389/fnhum.2018.00277. PMID: 30050418; PMCID: PMC6050388.